Not So Great Expectations

Mary,

With a prayer this
book blesses you!

Chris Deken

Not So Great Expectations

Don't Believe Everything You Think

Christine Deken

Xulon Press

Xulon Press
2301 Lucien Way #415
Maitland, FL 32751
407.339.4217
www.xulonpress.com

Paperback ISBN-13: 978-1-6322-1990-9
Ebook ISBN-13: 978-1-6322-1991-6

Dedication

To my husband, Kirk
and
To our children, Megan, Caitlin, Rory, Sean, Jillian,
and grandchildren
The joy of being your wife, mom, and grandma has exceeded
all my best expectations.

Acknowledgments

Nehemiah is the name we associate with the rebuilding of the Jerusalem wall after the exile, yet many people, named and unnamed were standing guard and building in the place where God had put them. So too with the building of this book. Only God knows the full contribution of others but I will attempt to acknowledge the substantial help I received risking that by mentioning some, others will be unmentioned. I take comfort in the knowledge that God knows perfectly and will reward your service which is infinitely better!

Thank you to my husband Kirk who unwaveringly supported me and this endeavor for many years and in many ways. Without you, this book would still be an idea. Thanks to Caitlin Ross and Rosy Talarzyk, early readers who endured a much less polished manuscript yet gave feedback and encouraged me to continue. Thanks to my longtime friend, Patrice McCormac, who first discussed expectations with me and continues to point me to God and his ways. Thank you to all the sisters in Christ in various Bible study groups who prayed for many years for this book. Your work in prayer is perhaps the greatest contribution. Thank you to later readers, Barbara Scott, Heidi Klingler, Craig Blazakis, Eric Schroer and Evan Williams and to Jillian Puchovich for input on the back cover. I valued your input and saw God at work through each of you. Thank you, Rory Deken of DekenDesigns for your work on the websites and patience with all my computer questions. Thank you Leah Doyle for using your artistic gift to help design the cover.

Thank you to Dwell Community Church, a ministry of XCF, for its emphasis on the word of God and commitment to and implementation of the biblical vision to equip every member for the work of service. Finally, thanks to all the students in the Not So Great Expectations class for your comments and contributions. You helped to refine this material.

Of course to God goes the greatest thanks. "LORD, you establish peace for us; all that we have accomplished you have done for us" (Isa. 26:12)

Table of Contents

Preface

Frequently, I find myself disappointed, discouraged, and despairing even when my circumstances in life are good. Upon closer examination, I discover the problem lies not in my circumstances but my thoughts. My thoughts about how life should operate or how someone should act have grown into expectations that are unrealistic, unmet, or just plain wrong. All too often, relationships in families, churches, employment, and communities become strained or even destroyed due to disappointed expectations. Although forming expectations of people, life, and God seem to be a natural human tendency, my search for a book comprehensively written on this topic from a Christian perspective turned up empty. Many Christian books discuss expectations in various areas of life, such as marriage, parenting, or God.[1] As I continued to consider this topic, I found passages in the Bible that demonstrated not-so-great expectations of both Old and New Testament characters. Because of the ultimate value God places on the importance of relationships, I began to see how wrong expectations certainly damage relationships and cause other kinds of destruction as well. Along with these biblical examples and my sense of the far-reaching and widespread cost that wrong expectations have caused in my own life, I became increasingly burdened to share these ideas.

I have approached this task by offering a broad overview of the topic of expectations. Initial chapters will define, distinguish, and clarify destructive expectations, as I offer examples from Scripture and other sources. Next, I will examine common but incorrect expectations of God and people. Impossibly high expectations of life, including those unique to Christians, will follow. Although this wide scope necessarily limits the depth of exploration, I hope that inspection of the most common expectations in many different relationships and situations will illuminate the subtle beliefs that have taken residence in our minds. This, in turn, will help us more quickly and readily recognize potentially damaging expectations in the specific situations of our individual lives. By way of resolution, I will offer tools to rehabilitate and renew our minds, and reasons to replace our misguided expectations with a secure and steadfast hope in God, who is the best and ultimate answer to destructive expectations.

Some qualifications are necessary. Expectations provide one lens through which to scrutinize our thoughts, one exercise to renew our minds. Also, much of this writing touches on gray areas and degrees of expectations which may arise according to an individual's season of life or unique circumstances. Feel free to turn to those expectations that are currently applicable to your life and to skip those less pertinent.

With a prayer for the Holy Spirit's help, I write that he will bring to awareness the destructive power of expectations and cause good to come of this endeavor. To God belongs the credit. *"All that we have accomplished, you have done for us"* (Isa. 26:12).

Chapter 1:
Introduction to Expectations

Don't Believe Everything You Think — Bumper Sticker

What are expectations? The word possesses a range of meanings. Webster's dictionary offers three definitions of "expect": to look forward; to suppose or think and; to consider probable or certain.[2] In the Bible, two Greek words are translated into variations of the word "expect": *ekdechomai* and *prosdokao*.

Prosdokao means to watch toward or to look for. This meaning is neutral and includes the idea of anticipation or looking forward to the future without any demand, similar to Webster's first definition of "expect." When we expect, we anticipate what is going to happen. For example, when planning for retirement, we discuss "life expectancy." When a woman is pregnant, we call her an "expectant mother." Often, when the future becomes the present, we acknowledge things did not turn out the way we had anticipated. In hindsight, our true expectations are revealed through despair and disappointment.

Ekdechomai, on the other hand, connotes a stronger, more forceful sense of *taking* to receive for oneself.[3] This word combines the ideas of Webster's second and third definitions, which describe expectations as thoughts we consider to be probable or certain. Our

1

judgments become so certain that we essentially begin to demand or take from others. Expectations understood in this negative way are the concerns of this book.

Harmful expectations are wrong thoughts or beliefs we accept as true but are often based on lies or unchallenged assumptions. Alongside a harmful expectation, a sense of demand or entitlement begins to fester. We assign our thoughts the weight of actual truth and hold God and others to these standards. Damage results when our ideas or thoughts become not-so-great expectations. This title was chosen not only for its playful twist on the novel *Great Expectations* by Charles Dickens, but also because the phrase distinguishes proper expectations and is ambiguous enough to include all the many ways our thoughts may go awry. Perhaps some examples can illuminate.

Charles Templeton had professed Christianity for most of his adult life. For many years, he accompanied Billy Graham on his evangelistic crusades, preaching the gospel to thousands. However, this once-very-active man for Jesus Christ bluntly stated he no longer believed in God.[4] To explain his reversal, he offered two reasons, one concerning the exclusivity of Jesus as the only way to God. He then simply stated his second reason: "I cannot believe in a God who allows suffering and evil to persist."

This issue concerning the problem of evil and suffering is very complex, and mankind has long pondered this dilemma. In no way do I presume to add to the discussion in any serious way, to minimize the pain or confusion of a suffering person, or even to suggest the issue can be reduced to one dimension. But the problem of evil and suffering contains an unchallenged assumption: that a loving, sovereign God prohibits the simultaneous existence of evil and suffering. Is this true? We feel certain that if we had the power, we would fix the pain of the world, and we expect that a good God would as well. By his admission, Templeton surveyed the evil and suffering in the world, and it caused him to renounce his faith. Perhaps his disappointed expectation that a loving God would fix evil and suffering played a part in deadening his relationship with God. In this example, Templeton's assumption, as I will argue later in detail, is just wrong.

Disappointed expectations affect not only our relationship with God but also our relationships with other people. For example, Kaylynn was married eighteen years when she discovered her husband's unfaithfulness. She tearfully expressed shock: "I never thought this would happen to us." When well-publicized statistics report the demise of many marriages due to unfaithfulness, why did she feel invulnerable to infidelity? Why did she have the confident expectation that her marriage was immune? Maybe Kaylynn was right to expect faithfulness. Is not faithfulness the essential promise in the marriage vows? If Kaylynn and her husband possessed a realistic expectation of human frailty and sinfulness, might it have helped prevent her husband's adultery?

Jack shrugged his shoulders in surrender as he contemplated the disappointing state of his marriage and admitted, "I never thought *marriage* would be like *this.*" What did he think marriage would be like? What was he hoping for that did not materialize? Were his expectations too high? Could Jack enjoy his marriage more if he examined or was aware of his unrealistic expectations?

Not-so-great expectations not only destroy marriages, but they often dismantle other family relationships as well. Susan hung up the phone and vowed she would never speak to her younger sister Mary again. Mary had forgotten once more to call on Susan's birthday or to ask about her chronically sick child. Mary never returned Susan's phone calls, and she only called when she wanted to talk about her own life and family. When the phone screen displayed her sister's name, Susan had not answered. Were Susan's unmet expectations worth the loss of her relationship with her sister?

Another family is broken apart by disappointed expectations after the death of their father. Elizabeth was the executor of their father's will. She followed the letter of the probate law and provided only the required communication about the disposition of the estate. Elizabeth's sister, Ellen, felt entitled to ongoing and frequent communications about the probate of the estate, and when communication was absent, she suspected collusion and theft among the other siblings. Were Ellen's expectations unreasonable? How many family members have become estranged, not because someone commits a moral or legal wrong, but because the high expectations of one were unmet?

Christians are not exempt from wrong expectations. The evening news reports a man was arrested for child molestation and adds that he was a teacher in the children's ministry of his church. Another story depicts protesting Christians spouting hateful words toward attendants at a military funeral. A women's Bible study conversation descends into mean-spirited gossip about an absent member. In all of these situations, a person might protest, "I wouldn't think a Christian would act like that!"

My own heart feels disappointment in the expectations I hold of myself; I continue to struggle to forgive a perceived offense or to relinquish evil thoughts toward another. I have been forgiven so much, so why can't I easily forgive others?

Daily, we are affected by wrong ideas about God, ourselves, or others that are untrue, unrealistic, or just plain wrong. Even in the small details of life, expectations exist. For every text message I send, I expect a response. A lack of response can fuel feelings of rejection and awaken desires to punish or withdraw from my friend. Yet, in the scheme of life, an ignored text is a small pain. Other unchecked expectations can inflict tremendous damage.

Thoughts

Since expectations begin in our thoughts, let us briefly consider them. God designed us to think. We are made in the image of God, and God thinks. In Genesis, God created through speech (Gen. 1:3). Speech is simply the verbal expression of thought. When we create dinner, negotiate a business contract, teach, or write, thought is presumed.

Psalm 139 explicitly tells us that God thinks of us. "How precious to me are your thoughts, God. How vast is the sum of them. Were I to count them, they would outnumber the grains of sand" (vv. 17-18). In another Psalm, David contemplates the magnificence of creation and marvels that God thinks of humans: "What is man that you are mindful of him, the son of man that you care for him?" (Ps. 8:4).

As part of God's original design for humans, thinking can be seen when God gave Adam the responsibility to name the animals. Eve also demonstrated thought before her disobedience. "When the woman saw that the fruit of the tree was good for food and pleasing to the eye and also desirable for gaining wisdom, she took some and ate it" (Gen. 3:6). Eve *evaluated* the fruit as nutritious and appetizing and *considered* that it might give her wisdom.

Because of this thought-filled choice to disobey, humankind fell from the Creator's original design. As descendants of that first act of rebellion, we inherited a nature that rejects God's leadership and insists we choose our own way.

This nature of rebellion has profoundly affected our thought life. We think independently of our Maker, and consequently, our thoughts might not reflect truth or reality. Yet, they *feel* certain and reliable. The proverb summarizes, "There is a way that *seems right* to a man" (Prov. 14:12; 16:25). Thoughts about people, relationships, and life become wrong expectations when they rise to a level of certainty and demand. However, we might confuse expectations with other similar ideas. Distinguishing damaging expectations from other related concepts may be helpful.

Distinctions

Vision

Expectations differ from vision. A teacher or parent might have been counseled to create high expectations of students or children. Research supports that students will achieve greater results if they are given higher standards for which to strive.[5] While the term *expectation* is often used this way, a more precise term is *vision*. In the context of encouragement, vision is the ability of one person to see and communicate the potential of another person and what that person can accomplish. Vision encourages a student's success through helping them "see" themselves achieving, which empowers them to move in a positive direction. For a Christian, vision includes God's enabling and transforming power, which is found in verses such as Romans 8:11: "And if the Spirit of him who raised Jesus from the dead is living in you, he who raised Christ from the dead will also give life to your mortal bodies through his Spirit who lives in you." By way of contrast, expectations go beyond positively encouraging future accomplishment and demands a person to act in a certain way. Vision says, "You can," while expectation says, "You should." Whenever we demand another person *should* act in a certain way or find ourselves devastated by another's actions or inactions, our expectations may reveal unhealthy codependency on people, which is a form of idolatry that will be considered in light of expectations.

Idolatry

Extreme distress from unmet expectations may expose idolatry, which involves the elevation of another person or circumstance to the place God deserves. Some disappointment naturally results from unmet expectations, but inordinate or devastating emotions might reveal that another person or a circumstance has assumed God's place in our lives. Since damaging expectations primarily arise from incorrect or unrealistic thinking, wrong expectations can occur without idolatry. However, when wrong thinking is coupled with desperation for another person to act in a particular way or for a specific outcome to occur, our high expectations might also expose an idol. Considering the previous example concerning text messages, most of us expect a prompt response after sending a text. Yet, there are many legitimate explanations why a person may not respond promptly. To demand a quick response to a text is an unreasonably high expectation. When our thoughts dictate a particular way in which another person should act and they do not act in that way, the resulting emotion reveals the extent that we are dependent on this person. The unmet expectation is the occasion which reveals the dependence. The last part of this book argues that God is the only one who can bear the weight of our desires and looking to another person is misplacing our desires and therefore idolatry. While wrong thinking may not always involve idolatry, when we elevate our thoughts as the highest and absolute truth, a lack of humility is always present.

Arrogance

In every destructive expectation is a thread of arrogance. When we carry expectations, we impose on another person *our* ideas of what they should or should not do. By holding others to expectations, we allow our views and perspectives to dominate the relationship. If the expectation is based on biblical truth, we can discuss what is right or wrong and perhaps even agree to respectfully disagree if that truth is unclear. But expectations most often occur in specific situations in which the Bible does not particularly speak. For example, the Bible commands us to be kind and compassionate to one another (Eph. 4:32). Therefore, if my Christian friends did not attend my brother's funeral, can I accuse them of being unkind and in violation of this biblical command? Perhaps to attend the funeral was one way to be kind, but to require another person to demonstrate kindness according to my expectations promotes my perspective as the only way. Thus, expectations subtly exalt my views, opinions, and standards and disregard the thoughts of others. Such a self-righteous attitude is the opposite of humility, the attitude so esteemed by God and important to successful relationships.

God's Commands

The previous example raises a question. What about the "one another" verses in the Bible? Why can we not expect other Christians to treat us as God has commanded? God's commands concern the treatment of other Christians, such as forgive one another, forebear with one another, and love one another. The answer is that *God* commanded these behaviors. Even though he decreed these actions out of his love for our good and the good of others, God is the only one to whom we owe the obedience of these commands.

In the context of David's adulterous affair with Bathsheba and the murder of her husband, Uriah, David states in Psalm 51:4, "Against you, you only, have I sinned and done what is evil in your sight." David's sins of adultery and murder were also committed against Bathsheba and Uriah, as well as perhaps many others, as David was a king charged to rightly lead people. Yet, the inspired and inerrant Word tells us that first and foremost, David's sins were against God. *Our* sins are first and foremost against God.

Grasping this perspective can be extremely helpful when considering expectations in relationships. If we apprehend that obedience of biblical commands is owed first to God in our vertical relationship with him, then such understanding diminishes any expectation we think is owed to us in our human horizontal relationships.

If we apprehend that obedience of biblical commands is owed first to God in our vertical relationship with him, then such understanding diminishes any expectation we think is owed to us in our human horizontal relationships.

Moreover, when we fail to live up to the expectations of others, we can experience peace, knowing God has already paid for our failures, has forgiven us, and views us as his beloved son or daughter. This view better orients our focus toward God rather than expectations of people.

In this life, relationships will inevitably be fraught with sin, hurt, and failure. But when each person in a relationship attempts to follow God regarding how he or she should act while at the same time not punishing others for their failures, joyful and durable relationships are possible.

Promises

An exception to the idea of maintaining low or no expectations of people may arise when promises are made, such as in marriage. In every Christian marriage, a couple makes a promise of faithfulness, so each spouse can rightly expect the other spouse to fulfill the promise. Other situations may legitimately engender expectations, for example, when parties agree to a set of commitments.[6]

Every legal contract involves promises. Employment involves reciprocal promises to perform work and to pay for the work performed. Friends may voluntarily agree to certain terms or parameters of their relationship. Many relationships involve promises or agreements, and we are entitled to rely on those. Our reliance, however, is within the overarching reality that we are all imperfect, sinful people this side of eternity, and our primary and ultimate hope must rest in our relationship with God.

Since our ultimate hope must rest in God, our beliefs about our relationship with him deserve the highest consideration. A common but wrong expectation about how to begin a relationship with God is the first belief we should consider.

Chapter 2:
The Deadliest Expectation

On judgment day many will say to me, Lord, Lord! We prophesied in your name and cast out demons in your name and performed many miracles in your name. But I will reply, I never knew you (Matt. 7:22–23, NLT).

A pervasive expectation of great harm sounds something like this: "When I die, God will accept me into His presence because I have been a 'good' person, or because I have performed good works that outweigh my bad choices, or because I have practiced rituals that make up for the wrongs I have committed."

According to God's Word, this common belief is wrong and directly opposite to the truth. The Bible compares our righteous acts to a holy God by describing them as "filthy rags" (Isa. 64:6).[7] In the New Testament, Paul writes, "All have sinned and fall short of the glory of God" (Rom. 3:23); "there is no one righteous, not even one, there is no one who understands, no one who seeks God ... not one does good"(Rom. 3:10–12; Eccl. 7:20). And these are just a few of the passages.

Anyone who holds the view that their good works will qualify them for God's kingdom will be turned away.

> *Not everyone who calls out to me, Lord, Lord, will enter the Kingdom of Heaven. Only those who actually do the will of my Father in heaven will enter. On judgment day many will say to me, Lord! Lord! We prophesied in your name and cast out demons in your name and performed many miracles in your name, But I will reply, I never knew you. Get away from me, you who break God's laws. (Matt. 7:21–23 NLT)*

To the people who offer good works of prophesying, casting out demons, miracles, or any similar good deeds, Jesus will reply, "I never knew you."

From a horizontal, human perspective, these people appeared religious and moral. They expected their good works and personal merit to warrant entrance into heaven. The stinging reply of Jesus still applies to anyone who offers their good works, morals, or rituals as evidence that they should be allowed entrance into heaven. The consequence of such a wrong expectation for the religious people Jesus addressed was eternal separation from God. This consequence is the same today. Jesus explained that only those who do the will of his Father will enter heaven. What does it mean to do the will of the Father? Would not doing God's will include performing good works or being a moral person? In John 6:29, Jesus stated clearly, "This is the only work God wants from you: Believe in the one he has sent" (NLT).

What does it mean to "believe" in the one God sent? Many think belief in Jesus consists of mental agreement with the truth that Jesus existed. Others accept the existence of Jesus and further agree that Jesus is who he claimed to be: the incarnate God, Messiah, and Savior of the world. However, even agreement with the divinity of Jesus is not saving faith. Jesus encountered a man possessed by an evil spirit who shouted, "What do you want with us, Jesus of

Nazareth? Have you come to destroy us? I know who you are—the Holy One of God" (Mark 1:24). The evil spirit recognized Jesus as "the Holy One of God," yet his belief did not save him.

In contrast, Peter's recognition of the identity of Jesus in John 6:68-69 indicates true belief. "Lord, to whom shall we go? You have the words of eternal life. We believe and know that you are *the Holy One of God*" (emphasis added). What is the difference? Both encounters identify Jesus as the Holy One of God, but only Peter's belief was able to save. The difference lies in Peter's response, which contained humility and trust. Peter knew not only who Jesus was but who *he* was in relation to Jesus. He knew he had nowhere else to go. He renounced any ability in himself to attain eternal life, trusting Jesus alone.

Belief in the biblical sense means more than intellectual assent to the identity of Jesus. Saving faith requires that one entrust himself to the work of Jesus on the Cross. The true believer is the one who has stopped appealing to his own merit, goodness, or actions and has entrusted his acceptance before God based solely on the work of Jesus. This difference in belief is beautifully illustrated in a parable.

> *To some who were confident of their own righteousness and looked down on everybody else, Jesus told this parable: Two men went up to the temple to pray, one a Pharisee and the other a tax collector. The Pharisee stood up and prayed about himself: "God, I thank you that I am not like other people—robbers, evildoers, adulterers—or even like this tax collector. I fast twice a week and give a tenth of all I get." But the tax collector stood at a distance. He would not even look up to heaven, but beat his breast and said, "God, have mercy on me, a sinner." I tell you that this man, rather than the other, went home justified before God."*
> *(Luke 18:9-14)*

In this parable, the tax collector's belief included humility. He understood that as a sinner, he had nothing to offer God except a request for mercy. The thief on the cross also demonstrated saving belief when he humbly admitted his sinfulness and simply asked Jesus, "Remember me when you come into your kingdom" (Luke 23:42). Jesus promised paradise to this thief, even though the thief had no good deeds or religious works to offer.

The belief in God that saves us involves a humble admission of our own unworthiness before the perfect holiness of God, and a willingness to ask for God's provision, which is Jesus. Saving faith then directly contradicts the "I am good enough" expectation.

If this belief persists in your mind, please consider it a worthwhile expenditure of time to further investigate God's Word, which explains true belief in Jesus.[8] If such a wrong expectation is never corrected, and God's provision of Jesus remains unaccepted, separation from God continues for all of eternity. No other wrong expectation causes greater damage.

Saving faith then directly contradicts the "I am good enough" expectation.

But most of us live in a bubble of many expectations. When this bubble bursts, we experience anger, disappointment, sadness, and hurt. In many cases, our relationship with God and others is irreparably damaged. The next chapter will further consider the damage from not-so-great expectations.

Chapter 3:
Harm from Not So Great Expectations

Expectation is the root of all heartache. — *Unknown*

Not-so-great expectations cause a variety of damage. Sometimes this damage is subtle and it can differ in kind and intensity. Certainly, relationships with God and other people are negatively affected by the damage.

A healthy relationship requires the freedom to choose to enter into the relationship, the extent of involvement within the relationship, and how to act in the relationship. Unrealistic expectations injure relationships in the sense that they usurp another person's freedom. Interestingly, one of the Greek words previously mentioned, translated in the New Testament as expect, suggests this harm. *Ekdechomai* connotes the sense of *taking* to receive for oneself.[9] When our expectations are demands, we *take* from a person. If we demand that friends act in a certain way, we have essentially constricted their freedom to choose how they act or respond, at least without repercussion or retaliation on our part. Inevitably, when a friend responds differently than we had expected, we may treat them to an emotional response ranging from rage to silent withdrawal.

We may even end the relationship. The proverb quoted earlier, "There is a way that seems right to a man," finishes with a warning: "but in the end it leads to death" (Prov. 14:12; 16:25).

We intuitively know relationships are risky, for we cannot make others perform as we desire. Knowing we cannot control how others treat us produces fear and may cause us to attempt to control indi-

*He gives each of us the dignity of choice
to enter a love relationship with him.*

viduals through burdensome expectations. God's dealings with us provides a model for healthy relationships, which demonstrates that trying to control others through expectations is destructive.

God created us as free will-choosing beings with the potential to enter a mutual love relationship with him. By definition, a love relationship requires people to choose whether to be in the relationship at all, how much or how little to invest in the relationship, and how to act and respond to one another. In so creating us, God risked rejection and other horrific consequences. Although much is at stake, God did not and will not force any human to relate to him, even though he has the right to do so as the Creator. He gives each of us the dignity of choice to enter a love relationship with him.

Furthermore, once we open the door to a relationship with God through Jesus Christ, he does not dictate or demand how we live out that relationship. He calls us to obey and follow him, often giving us clear directions for our part in the relationship. Yet, God does not hold us hostage to his commands or sever the relationship when we fail to fulfill our part. If God does not force us to act a certain way when, as our Maker, he has every right to do so, then neither should we force or expect others to act in a certain way in our relationships with them.

However, one healthy expectation that should be present in all human relationships is the expectation that all persons should be treated with dignity. This is true because all humans possess dignity as image-bearers of God. Abuse in all its forms is a legitimate and important reason to end a relationship. Apart from abuse, which definitively destroys relationships, not-so-great expectations cause needless relational damage. In certain situations, expectations can also be dangerous.

Comparatively less important than relationships, driving a car with high expectations may prove hazardous as well. To expect drivers to follow the rules of the road might seem reasonable, yet, while a driver may sometimes obey the letter of the law, this driver might still not meet the expectations of other drivers. Road rage has too often ended in unnecessary destruction or death from a high expectation of driving perfection. When anger escalates to such a level, other issues are likely simmering inside a person. But expectations may also be involved, as a true example in my life illustrates.

A long time ago, I was a passenger while my boyfriend was driving on a fairly narrow side street in our city. While awaiting clearance to turn left into a busy, four-lane main thoroughfare, my boyfriend stopped in the middle of the road, and he did not pull over enough to the right. A driver in a very large, old, dilapidated car turned into this side street and nearly hit our car. The driver reacted in anger, stopped his car, and started yelling at my boyfriend. When my boyfriend began to get out of the car (I'm not sure why), I heard the offended driver's elderly female passenger yell, "Get the gun, Wilbur!" I then saw Wilbur reach back onto the shelf under the rear window and grab the longest-looking rifle I had ever seen. Whereupon my boyfriend, in one motion, slid back into the car, stepped on the gas, and without looking, sped across the four-lane crossroad to escape being shot.

This true and currently humorous story reveals some nearly fatal expectations at work. Wilbur expected to have more of the road available for his turn, so he became angry. My boyfriend was not expecting a rifle confrontation over the issue. I was assuming an uneventful drive home. But even where there are rules, laws, and agreements, such as in driving, can we legitimately expect these rules or other driving courtesies will always be followed? Each day, the number of accidents in any city would tell us differently. An appropriate expectation is that other drivers, myself included, will intentionally or unintentionally violate the rules of the road. If we maintained a more accurate view, assuming mistakes will be made, we all could drive more calmly and be less likely to engage in conflict that ends in road rage.

Although not usually life-threatening, expectations can cause unnecessary personal sadness and crush our joy. Michael J. Fox, an actor likely best known for his role in *Back to the Future* and now suffering from Parkinson's disease, stated, "My happiness grows in direct proportion to my acceptance and in inverse proportion to my expectations."[10] We can be emotionally weighed down solely from unmet or unrealistic expectations. Not-so-great expectations can cause grumbling and negatively rule the undercurrent of our emotional state. While we cannot attain perfect or permanent joy in this life, unmet or wrong expectations can rob us of much joy we could experience. Other types of damage may result, which will be mentioned in specific examples.

Yet, how do we know if wrong expectations are contributing to a lack of joy or causing other damage? How do we discern and unearth the less obvious but errant expectations which are the root cause of this damage?

Chapter 4:
Discernment of Expectations

Search me, God, and know my heart; test me and know my anxious thoughts (Ps. 139:23).

Discernment of not-so-great expectations generally involves developing greater self-awareness in these following five areas.

Emotions

Emotions, such as anger, hurt, and disappointment, often reveal wrong expectations. Our emotions are perhaps the best window into our soul. They uncover what we think and what is truly important to us. However, discerning precise emotions may be easier for some than others. Some may recognize they are feeling angry; some may know they are upset but cannot identify their specific emotion. Still, others completely deny negative emotions. The exercise of examining our emotions is exemplified in Psalms 42 and 43. The Psalmist asks, "Why are you downcast, O my soul? Why so disturbed within me?" (42:5, 11; 43:5). When our emotions are barking at us, we may need to pause and attempt to specifically identify what we are feeling.

19

After identifying emotions, we must backpedal from those emotions to our thoughts. Days after my brother's funeral, in addition to the sadness and grief over his death, I was feeling hurt. Only much later did I sort out that my hurt feelings arose from the certain but unmet expectation that some of my Christian friends would come to the funeral home.

Often, disappointed expectations result from omission; we are angry or hurt because another person *failed* to do what we expected. When I call someone and they do not return the call after an extended period, my anger reveals that assumption. Others may believe a return call is optional. Maybe returning phone calls is an implicit agreement of friendship; maybe it is not. Our emotions can tell us which way we view the unreturned phone call.

Frustration from car or appliance breakdowns may uncover an expectation that man-made machines should never break. When plans are thwarted or unplanned expenses arise, frustration is normal. But when the strength of our emotions seems disproportionate to the mishap, an unrealistic expectation may be the cause of our frustration.

Thoughts

Although intertwined with emotions, our thoughts alone may highlight our expectations. While many are aware of their thoughts, others do not examine them at all. Even the naturally self-aware person may need to occasionally ask, "What am I thinking right now? What is causing me to act or feel this way?" Uprooting foundational expectations is an exercise in walking backward. In this process, we examine our behavior and emotions and then consider what this scrutiny uncovers. To identify the thought behind the emotions, we might ask a "why" question, such as, "Why am I sad, hurt, or angry?" or "What *precisely* is bothering me?" Not all answers to negative emotions will be wrong or unmet expectations. Yet, many times the answer to these questions will be untrue or unfulfilled expectations.

In my soccer mom years, many parents forcefully disagreed with the referee's call. They screamed and fitfully paced the sidelines with clenched fists. When I once felt my anger rise at a referee's judgment call, I asked, "What is my expectation of a soccer referee? Is it that a human entrusted with the rules of soccer will accurately interpret and apply them one hundred percent of the time?" After mentally verbalizing these questions, I realized my wrong expectation. God's Word tells us that every human falls short of perfection. His verdict helped me evaluate my incorrect thinking. Should we hold any human to perfection in whatever work he is engaged? Or, is the better way to think as follows: a referee with superior knowledge of the rules of soccer will sometimes make a wrong call *or* a call with which I disagree since I too am biased. Such a judgment call by a fallible human is nevertheless an essential part of the game of soccer. My thoughts revealed an expectation of perfection of soccer referees and possibly also an idol of the game of soccer. Expectations of perfection of any human, whether a referee, a driver, or a church leader, are always wrong.

Speech

Another way to discern expectations, in addition to thoughts and emotions, is through listening to our words when we hear ourselves repeat phrases like, "I thought this would happen," or "You should have done this." *I thought* and *you should* seem to be key phrases to alert us to expectations. "I was supposed to ..." is another phrase that might disclose disappointed plans. When her husband changed jobs and she found herself moving across the country, my friend Paula heard herself saying, "I was supposed to continue living in the same city for the rest of my life." Then a cancer diagnosis post-poned those plans. She heard herself again saying, "*I was supposed to* have moved by now."

Speech in the form of grumbling or criticizing may reveal not-so-great expectations. Upon completion of our tax forms, my criticism about the tax system to my husband was a veiled but disappointed expectation of paying fewer taxes that year. My verbal expression of complaint exposed the real reason, which was personal disappoint-ment in our projected tax outcome, not against the IRS.

Others

We can uncover our expectations by not only listening closely to our speech but articulating our thoughts with others, particularly for those who are less self-aware. Sometimes we need help from others to see inside ourselves. Jeremiah 17:9 states, "The heart is deceitful above all things and beyond cure. Who can understand it?" When we share with others our thoughts, feelings, and grum-blings about the events and concerns in our lives, they may detect the inner stuff of expectations. Our friends may recognize within us a high expectation of another person, or they may be able to offer a perspective from God's Word on a situation that we are unable or unwilling to see. God has blessed us with each other for many rea-sons, but to support and encourage each other in the transforma-tion of our unbiblical expectations certainly is an advantage from which we can profit.

God's Word and Spirit

Finally, as God's children indwelt by his Spirit, we have his help to apply his Word to each situation and to know our hearts. Often, we will need the supernatural help of the Holy Spirit to grasp the muck in our hearts. This avenue of discernment is particularly important and superior to the other ways we have covered thus far, since only God knows us fully. Only God is infallible; therefore, only he can perfectly see the truth in our hearts and minds. After David celebrates God's extensive knowledge of him throughout Psalm 139, David finishes the psalm with a prayer for God to expose his hurtful ways. Like David, as we scrutinize our thoughts, emotions, and speech, we need to continually pray for God's Spirit to expose our not-so-great expectations. Through clarity from the Holy Spirit, we have hope to recognize our wrong thinking and be transformed.

Chapter 5:
Sources of Not So Great Expectations

Ideas, like large rivers, never have just one source.
— *Willy Ley*

Understanding the sources that give rise to expectations may contribute to further discernment. Realizing why we believe a certain way or unquestionably accept some ideas may help us recognize our not-so-great expectations.

Recurrent Events

Life consists of much regularity: the sunrise and sunset; the seasons; birth, growth, and death. When events in nature recur, we expect they will continue. For example, in Acts 28:6, when Paul received a snakebite, the witnesses naturally expected him to swell up and die. In the first century, poisonous bites would likely result in death. The islanders possessed a legitimate expectation based on nature. Therefore, when Paul did not die, they believed he was supernatural: a god.

Other recurrent events beyond nature might give rise to expectations. When people regularly act a certain way, we believe they will always act that way. My husband's business requires that he travel throughout our state a couple of days a week. On those travel days, he calls home when he stops for lunch. This daily practice began many years ago and still continues. What began as a wonderfully nice gesture on his part quickly became a definite expectation on mine. One day, when I had not heard from him hours after lunch, I began to worry. I imagined a traffic accident, an abduction at a gas station, or some other horror. When my husband arrived home and did not explain, my worry then turned to disappointment, and I began to silently punish him by withdrawing. Subsequently, I realized I had developed the unreasonable expectation that my husband would never fail to call on travel days. Only then was I able to be gracious and thankful when he arrived home safely on days when he forgot to call. An event that happens regularly gives rise to an expectation that it will recur.

Promises

Another source of expectations arises when a promise is made. Is it acceptable to develop an expectation when someone makes a promise? The answer depends on who is making the promise. If a human makes a promise, the weakness and sinfulness of fallen humans must influence the expectation. For any number of reasons, from simple forgetfulness to intentional mistreatment, humans will fail to keep their promises. Shakespeare stated, "Oft expectation fails, and most oft there, Where most it promises."[11]

When friends make a promise, it may be legitimate to expect they will follow through, but within the overarching understanding of their imperfect humanness. We must leave room in our relationships for people to fail to live up to the promises they have made with the best of intentions—and be thankful when others overlook our failed promises.

Family Taught

Another source of expectation arises from our families. According to our unique upbringings, we instinctively expect life to be ordered in a certain way. Conflicting expectations surface when a couple marries or begins to have children. For example, new parents bring different experiences of how their parents disciplined or failed to discipline them. These dif-

We must leave room in our relationships for people to fail to live up to the promises they have made with the best of intentions—and be thankful when others overlook our failed promises.

ferent experiences can produce vastly different expectations within the couple concerning the discipline of their young children. Many other expectations may be family-generated, concerning household chores, holidays, or finances.

In my family, my mom cooked and cleaned, while my dad worked outside the home. By the time I was an adult, the generational expectation that every woman would stay home and perform the household chores while the man would work outside the home had given way to many different ideas of making family life work. For a time, I worked as an attorney while also raising children. When our third child was born, I chose to primarily undertake the household and child-rearing duties from home while also writing occasionally for a legal publication. Two years later, our twins were born. With five children under nine years old, I could no longer complete the weekly chore of nineteen loads of laundry. My husband would periodically pitch in and try to wash, dry, and fold a couple of the loads, yet his help would elicit an angry reaction within my heart.

For many years, I criticized how my husband did the laundry, noticing that he put white clothes in with darks or permanent-press clothing in with towels. He understandably became frustrated that I met his sincere attempts to help with anger and criticism. I tried to be thankful that he was helping, but every time he aided me with the laundry, I seemed unable to respond with anything but negative emotions. After many years of this repeated relational cycle of conflict over the laundry, I finally prayed for God to help me understand what was in my heart, which made me unable to cheerfully accept my husband's help. Shortly after this prayer, my husband carried a load of freshly laundered towels up from the basement. I would not usually criticize a load of towels, but feelings of anger erupted once again. Then I realized if my husband was doing the laundry, I felt I had failed at running the household. He could cook and help with child care, but if he did laundry, my identity as a successful homemaker was shaken. Where did I get such an expectation of myself, especially in modern times of equal labor? I suspect the source was my family upbringing. My mom *always* did the laundry, while my dad *never* did.

The realization that I was carrying an unreasonable expectation of myself, that I was basing my worth on being able to accomplish this household chore, was helpful to our marriage. I expressed this wrong expectation to my husband, sharing that I had developed the idea that if he did the laundry, I was a failure. We laughed at the silliness of basing my worth on such shaky ground. After our conversation, he understood my irrational anger a little better, and together, we experienced a moment of God's grace, knowing God had exposed the deep source of an ongoing though a minor conflict in our marriage. As a side note, my husband still occasionally launders his clothes or towels, and I occasionally continue to struggle with feelings of failure; however, I try to smile and express my gratitude for his help. I silently remind myself that my worth is based on my identity as a child of God alone.

Culture/World System

In addition to family backgrounds, cultural differences may create destructive expectations. Over time, missionaries have learned the importance of understanding cultural differences. The following true missionary account illustrates critically different social expectations. Two single women set out to translate the Bible into the unwritten language of a tribal village. Initially, these women were well received, and it appeared their mission would be successful. However, once settled, the women established a morning routine of porch sitting while reading their Bibles and sipping lime juice in the hot, muggy climate. The villagers began to avoid them, soon becoming relationally cold and completely unwilling to help in the translation. After months of this treatment, the missionaries left, and others discovered the misunderstanding. In that tribe, lime juice was considered a "morning-after contraceptive." The villagers had assumed the unmarried women had engaged in sexual intercourse the night before. Drinking lime juice in the morning ruined their reputation with the villagers! [12]

Much has been written concerning cultural differences that are beyond the scope of this writing. To learn about differences in culture to achieve better communication and harmony in a relationship is an act of love. Christians especially would want to avoid needless harm and conflict that may occur through different expectations that are based on cultural norms.

Media

Cultural expectations may be communicated through the media, which itself creates expectations, many of which are incorrect. Media, including television, magazines, movies, and the internet, may create false expectations. Many images that various forms of media project, do not depict life accurately. Magazine photographs are airbrushed; lumps, bumps, and wrinkles are ironed smooth. Television depicts families in which conflicts are resolved in less than twenty minutes, and crimes are solved in under an hour. These images or ideas may unconsciously become expectations, even when we know the pictures have been altered and the shows are fictitious. Research has revealed one example in the connection between the amount of media an individual consumes and body image problems. "Overall media consumption is a positive predictor of eating disorder and body image dissatisfaction."[13] While many causes contribute to eating disorders, the media is culpable through the projection of unattainable expectations concerning our bodies.

Media messages may also drive high expectations for the American dream, claiming a large, beautiful house, a new car with a few children, and a successful career to be the definition of a good life. Facebook posts of only our best moments create illusions and unrealistic expectations that life is a full-time vacation. Additional sources may foster wrong expectations beyond what has been mentioned. Since much of the Bible records the history of humankind and expectations are common to humans, the Bible provides examples.

Chapter 6:
Biblical Examples

For my thoughts are not your thoughts, neither are your ways my ways, declares the Lord (Isa. 55:8).

Naaman and Gehazi

In 2 Kings 5, Naaman is a biblical character with not-so-great expectations. He was the commander of the army of the king of Aram and was suffering from leprosy. His wife's servant girl reported that a prophet in Samaria might be able to cure him. With a letter from the king of Aram, Naaman traveled to the king of Israel and asked for healing. When Elisha, the prophet, heard the king of Israel had torn his robes in distress at Naaman's request, he requested Naaman to come to him. When Naaman appeared at Elisha's door, he sent a messenger with these directions: "Go wash yourself seven times in the Jordan, and your flesh will be restored and you will be cleansed" (2 Kgs. 5:10).

Despite the promise of healing, Naaman stalked away and angrily responded, "I thought that he would surely come out to me and stand and call on the name of the Lord his God, wave his hand over the spot and cure me of my leprosy! Are not the Abana and the Pharpar, the rivers of Damascus, better than any of the waters of Israel? Couldn't I wash in them and be cleansed?" (2 Kgs. 5:11–12).

Naaman held two expectations: first, how the healing would occur; second, that Elisha would personally tend to him. Naaman felt that Elisha's impersonal message was disrespectful, since Naaman was highly regarded in his own country. His pride in himself and his country was injured. However, Naaman's officers persuaded him to follow Elisha's easy instructions, challenging his prideful expectations. Because Naaman listened to his officers and followed Elisha's instructions, he was healed. If Naaman had stubbornly persisted in his own way of thinking, he would have remained leprous.

Another character in this account exhibited a wrong expectation. Elisha's servant, Gehazi, thought Elisha should have accepted Naaman's offering of gratitude. "Then Naaman and all his attendants went back to the man of God. He stood before him and said, 'Now I know that there is no God in all the world except in Israel. Please accept now a gift from your servant.' The prophet answered, 'As surely as the LORD lives, whom I serve, I will not accept a thing.' And even though Naaman urged him, he refused" (2 Kgs. 5:15–16). Gehazi thought contrary to Elijah. "Gehazi ... said to himself, 'My master was too easy on Naaman, this Aramean, by not accepting from him what he brought'" (5:20). Despite Elisha's explicit refusal, Gehazi acted on his expectation and greed. He trailed Naaman on his way back to Aram and lied to obtain the gift meant for Elisha. Gehazi returned to Elisha, who knew what Gehazi had done. When Gehazi lied again to Elisha, he was struck with leprosy.

Both characters, Naaman and Gehazi, expressed great certainty in their expectations despite the words of Elisha, a prophet of God. They trusted their thoughts instead of the Word of God through Elisha. Yet, their outcomes ended differently. Naaman, persuaded by his friends to follow Elisha's way, was healed. Gehazi acted without any counsel. With more confidence in his way of thinking than respect for Elisha, an agent of God, Gehazi became leprous. This story instructs us to examine our thoughts, even when we feel certain they are right, and to humbly seek counsel and input from God's Word and others.

A third character in this story, the king of Israel, illustrated the point of view of a person subject to an unrealistic expectation. The Israelite servant girl told Naaman's wife that a *prophet* could heal her husband. Yet, the king of Aram sent a letter requesting the king of Israel to heal Naaman: "With this letter I am sending my servant Naaman to you so that you may cure him of his leprosy" (2 Kgs. 5:6).

> Relationships crumble under the weight of expectations that are too high.

The king of Israel's response demonstrates the crushing weight of expectations that are too high. "As soon as the king of Israel read the letter, he tore his robes and said, 'Am I God? Can I kill and bring back to life? Why does this fellow send someone to me to be cured of his leprosy? See how he is trying to pick a quarrel with me?'" (2 Kgs. 5:7). The king of Israel recognized the pressure of being in the place where only God belongs. From this story, we can see that lofty expectations of others put imperfect and inadequate humans in the place of God, where no human can deliver. Relationships crumble under the weight of expectations that are too high.

Moses, David, and Goliath

Although Naaman's story is the most comprehensive biblical example of not-so-great expectations, many other Old Testament narratives expose misguided expectations as well. Moses thought God should have chosen a more eloquent spokesman (Exod. 4:10). If he had staunchly refused to trust God's view of his adequacy,

Moses would have missed the opportunity for God to use him. Goliath expected an experienced soldier with great weapons to fight him. "Am I a dog that you come at me with sticks?" (1 Sam. 17:43). Both Moses and Goliath illustrated a natural human expectation, which evaluates usefulness to God based on physical appearance or giftedness. Goliath lost his life for underestimating his enemy. In contrast, David righteously expected God would come through, and his thoughts focused on God's ability. "The Lord who delivered me from the paw of the lion and the paw of the bear will deliver me from the hand of this Philistine" (1 Sam. 17:37).

Despite our tendency to view usefulness to God based on external measures, God most often used fallible and ordinary people. Jesus's disciples were considered ordinary and uneducated (Acts 4:13). Timothy was young and timid (1 Tim. 4:12). Gideon was the youngest in his family and a member of the weakest clan (Judg. 6:15). Even Paul, exceptionally gifted and suited for ministry, expressed that his abilities were less relevant than God's empowerment. "Not that we are competent in ourselves to claim anything for ourselves, but our competence comes from God" (2 Cor. 3:5). Our assumptions are not God's thoughts or ways (Isa. 55:8). Based on these biblical examples, a correct expectation and encouraging thought for all is that God will use ordinary vessels to display His power. "But we have this treasure in jars of clay to show that this all-surpassing power is from God and not from us" (2 Cor. 4:7).

Messianic Expectations

In the New Testament era, perhaps the most prevalent incorrect expectation of the Jewish people concerned the Messiah. "Everyone was expecting the Messiah to come soon and they were eager to know whether John might be the Messiah" (Luke 3:15, NLT). Although scholars debate the nature and variety of first-century messianic expectations, the Samaritan woman at the well expressed her expectation. "I know that Messiah (called Christ) is coming. When he comes, he will explain everything to us" (John 4:25). She thought the Messiah would provide understanding. Jesus fulfilled her expectation when he explained "everything" about her hidden promiscuity.

Another expectation for the Messiah is expressed in John 12:34. "We have heard from the Law that the Christ will remain forever, so how can you say, 'The Son of Man must be lifted up'? Who is this 'Son of Man?'" This crowd's expectation of the Messiah did not include his death.

Another common expectation of the first century was that the Messiah would rescue Israel from its Roman oppressors and establish a peaceful reign as in the days of Israel's kingly glory. Among all the various expectations of the Messiah, none revealed humiliation and suffering.[14] To the disciples, Jesus had to repeatedly revise their expectations to include that he would suffer and die (Luke 9:22; 17:25; 22:15; 24:26, 46). "From that time on Jesus began to explain to his disciples that he must go to Jerusalem and suffer many things at the hands of the elders, chief priests and teachers of the law and that he must be killed and on the third day be raised to life" (Matt. 16:21).

Peter's expectation of a non-suffering Messiah was so strong that he rebuked Jesus. "Never, Lord! This shall never happen to you!" (Matt. 16:22). Judas likely held these expectations of the Messiah as well. Peter later revised his expectations, while Judas did not. Judas acted on his wrong expectation, which led to a betrayal of Jesus and his own suicide.

On the road to Emmaus, before Jesus disclosed himself to them, two of his followers expressed their disappointment: "But we had hoped that he was the one who was going to redeem Israel" (Luke 24:21). Even after the resurrection, the expectation for an immediate reigning king continued. "So when they met together, they asked him, 'Lord, are you at this time going to restore the kingdom to Israel?'"(Acts 1:6). The persistence of the apostles' expectation for a reigning, powerful Messiah was understandable, due in part to the many Old Testament predictions that indicated the Messiah would triumph and usher in world peace. They did not understand the Messiah would come twice: as a suffering servant and later as a reigning king. The expectations of Peter and the rest of the apostles for a triumphant, powerful ruler were revised only after the indwelling of the Holy Spirit.

Sometimes we have correct expectations that are rooted in the Bible but a limited or incorrect understanding of the facts. The Jewish people correctly knew from Scripture that the Messiah would descend from David and come from Bethlehem. They did not know, however, that Jesus was born in Bethlehem; they only knew of his upbringing in Galilee (John 7:41–42). They missed that Jesus had fulfilled the requirement as a descendant of David.

These examples demonstrate wrong or low expectations of God that biblical characters held, and they remind us to hold our ideas and perceptions loosely. Let us now consider how we too swim in a pool of incorrect expectations of God.

Chapter 7: Not So Great Expectations of God

You are seeing things merely from a human point of view, not from God's (Mark 8:33, NLT).

Not-so-great expectations about God perhaps prove most destructive to our lives. What do we think about God? Do we limit our thoughts to what he has revealed about himself? Or do we create ideas and expectations of God based on human understanding? As previously mentioned, Charles Templeton expected that an all-powerful God would not permit evil and suffering, and many embrace this assumption. It feels right. Deep inside us resides a strong sense of justice. Yet, on earth, we see only a small part of the larger picture. God addressed issues of innocent suffering, as well as his nature and character, in the book of Job, wherein Job and his friends expressed inaccurate expectations of God.

Job, though a "blameless and upright" man who "feared God and shunned evil"(Job 1:1), lost his children, livestock, and physical health. Attempting to make sense of such a horrible tragedy, his friends tenaciously expressed their belief that Job's suffering was the result of God's judgment of his sin. Eliphaz argued, "Consider now: Who, being innocent, has ever perished? Where were the upright ever destroyed? As I have observed, those who plow evil and those who sow trouble reap it" (Job 4:7-8). His conclusions were based on how he had "observed" life to work, not on what God has revealed. Bildad charged, "Does God pervert justice? Does the Almighty pervert what is right? When your children sinned against him, he gave them over to the penalty of their sin" (Job 8:3–4).

Job, in contrast, did not think he could explain God. He seemed to possess a deeper sense of humility. "How can a mortal be righteous before God? Though one wished to dispute with him, he could not answer him one time out of a thousand" (Job 9:2–3). Job did, however, ask what he had done wrong. "I will say to God: Do not condemn me, but tell me what charges you have against me" (Job 10:2). God eventually responded to Job but did not explain why he had to endure such heartbreak. Instead, God expanded Job's understanding of God himself. "Where were you when I laid the earth's foundations? Who marked off its dimensions? Have you comprehended the vast expanses of the earth? Can you raise your voice to the clouds and cover yourself with a flood of water? Who endowed the heart with wisdom or gave understanding to the mind?" (Job 38:4, 5, 18, 34, 36). God's challenges to Job seem designed to help him realize he possessed a fundamentally wrong expectation: that human creatures could fully understand God and his actions or inactions.

Although God has revealed much about himself in ways we can know and understand, much remains beyond full human comprehension, including innocent suffering and the persistence of evil, with which Charles Templeton and others struggle. In *Walking with God through Pain and Suffering,* Timothy Keller exposes a flawed assumption in the "problem of evil" argument. "If God is infinitely knowledgeable, why couldn't he have morally sufficient reasons for allowing evil that you can't think of? To insist that we know as much about life and history as an all-powerful God is a logical fallacy howsoever much the immanent frame of our culture would incline us to think that way." [15]

God's response to Job may prove helpful as we examine our logical fallacies and unconscious expectations of God. First, we can only know about God what he has expressly revealed to us. All other ideas about him must be held lightly and tentatively. Moreover, we should not expect that we will understand him fully. We are like children before God, always with an incomplete and immature understanding of him and his purposes. Yet, when we feel hurt or angry while suffering, we can cry out to our wise Father for understanding. Moses and the Psalmist felt the freedom to question God why in the midst of suffering (Exod. 5:22; Ps. 42:9). God may give us understanding or remind us of his sovereignty or past faithfulness. Or we may not hear a word. Such is God's prerogative. To suggest we know with certainty what God should or should not do in a specific situation, including instances of great evil or suffering, is presumptuous.

In the veiled arrogance of expectation, we might be asking the wrong question. Should not we rather ask, "Why has God been so good to give us life at all?" or "Why did God rescue rebellious creatures at the cost of His only beloved Son?" Elihu seems to hint at this. "But no one says, Where is God my Maker, who gives songs in the night, who teaches more to us than to the beasts of the earth and makes us wiser than the birds of the air?" (Job 35:10-11). Evil and suffering are complicated and perplexing issues, yet to conclude that God is not loving or nonexistent asserts an assumption beyond our knowledge.

What other not-so-great expectations of God do we commonly entertain? Some expect God to act as a personal genie; to make life easy. Others may fear a relationship with God will rob them of fun or the "good" life. Others who have never personally experienced God might reason he is uninvolved and distant. If the wrong ideas about God remain hidden and unexamined, damage will occur. Misinformed people often reject a personal relationship with a god who is far different than the God revealed in the Bible. The implications and potential damage of a few common misconceptions about God follow.

God Exists to Meet My Desires: The Genie God

How does this expectation of God manifest itself? When the overwhelming bulk of our prayers involve asking God to orchestrate life according to our desires, such prayers are directed to a god in a genie bottle.

It is not wrong to pray for life to go well. The apostle John prayed for Gaius. "Dear friend, I pray that you may enjoy good health and that all may go well with you, even as your soul is getting along well" (3 John 2). Like a good father, God delights when we talk to him and ask him for what we need and want. "Yet the Lord longs to be gracious to you; he rises to show you compassion" (Isa. 30:18).

God's Word also encourages us to boldly persist in prayer (Luke 18:1). However, if the content of our prayers over time reveals an excessive emphasis on requests and little or no praise and thanksgiving for what God has already done, this disparity may suggest a hidden expectation within us that God exists to merely make our lives better. Or, we may recognize this expectation through strong emotions that erupt when persistent petitions continue unanswered.

A sense of entitlement from God may increase subtly for the Christian. "I'm trying to follow you, God, so you should bless me, pave a smooth path ahead, and not let anything go wrong according to my agenda." The Psalmist expected better circumstances than the wicked. He writes, "Did I keep my heart pure for nothing? Did I keep myself innocent for no reason? I get nothing but trouble all day long; every morning brings me pain" (Ps. 73:13-14, NLT).

Under an inaccurate expectation or belief, God becomes small. He is seen as an indulgent grandpa, a compliant boss, or an impersonal vending machine made to dispense blessings. Moreover, when God is understood in this way, he becomes controllable and made in our image. Do our prayer duty and out pops a blessing.

God is the giver of all good things (Jas. 1:17), but he is much more. He may be more interested in our character development than good life circumstances because our characters will remain in eternity. God wants more for us: to be like his Son and gain glory from him and for him (2 Cor. 3:18). God may understand we need to know him better or depend on him far more than temporary pleasantries of life. Essentially, the god in the genie bottle is no different than a pagan idol made to appease. The true God of the Bible cannot and will not be reduced or contained. Perhaps that is why he questioned Job instead of answering him; he is not answerable to us.

Our prayers will never be wholly pure and without mixed motives. But with a correct view of God, we can grow to the place where our asking is rightly contextualized, such as David's prayer in Psalm 27:4: "One thing I ask of the Lord, this is what I seek: that I may dwell in the house of the Lord all the days of my life."

Because the Bible contains David's writings, we know he asked God for many things; deliverance, relief from distress, mercy, vindication, and safety are just a sampling of his requests. Yet, David's prayer reveals an understanding that to remain relationally close to God is the best circumstance. If we, like David, understood God in all his magnificence, our prayers for good life circumstances would occur in the context of humility for the mere privilege to dwell in God's presence and with an abundance of gratitude for blessings already received.

However, even if we begin our relationship with the right understanding of God, our thoughts can wander off course. David's son, Solomon, illustrated this possibility. Solomon initially prayed for the wisdom and knowledge to serve God and his people well (2 Chron. 1:10). This God-centered request pleased God, who then bestowed upon Solomon wealth, power, and peace in addition to wisdom. Through Solomon, we see the irony that sometimes God's good gifts insulate us, and we forget our blessings came from God's hand. Or, the blessings inflate a sense of self-security and create the illusion that we no longer need God. We may say, "We've got life taken care of; thank you very much." We forget we exist for God. Therefore, whatever he has given should be enjoyed but held loosely and offered back for His work and His glory. But for God's generosity, we would have nothing ... because "he himself gives all men life and breath and everything else" (Acts 17:25). Every literal breath is a gift from God.

If allowed to continue, the wrong expectation that God exists to indulge us will ultimately destroy our relationship with him. We cannot trust a God made in the image of humans, for we know humans are not trustworthy. If we cannot trust God to do what we demand in a particular area, we will begin to suspect he is untrustworthy in general. It would be difficult to then surrender control and approach him with our deepest fears and anxieties. We *want* his blessings, what he can give us, yet we *need* him. "My flesh and my heart may fail, but God is the strength of my heart and my portion forever" (Ps. 73:26).

I once overheard someone say, "I used to follow God, but then he let me down." We can empathize with this disappointment. But what was this person thinking? Was following God a matter of God doing what this person expected? When amid deep disappointments, the truth of God's prerogative to grant or deny our desires may seem cold and unloving. It is likely not the ideal time to expose a person's wrong expectations of God. Allowing others to express their hurts and disappointment toward God can be helpful, but eventually, we need to remember the truth.

God Will Rob Me of a Good Life

Due to fear, some refuse the free offer of God for a personal relationship with him; they fear if they surrender to God, he will deprive them of what they need or their idea of a "good" life. Fear of a personal relationship with God may be based on the false belief that God will take rather than give. One might think, "If I accept this free gift of salvation, what might God want from me? He might want to mess me over, take me somewhere I do not want to go, or make me do something I do not want to do."

We may fear change, for we may feel comfortable in our current state. To enter a relationship with the God who spoke the universe into existence would be quite a change. Sometimes Christians, though we possess knowledge of the goodness of God, also entertain this fear. We often play it safe, willing to accept easy tasks but unwilling to risk what is near to our hearts. Our fear indicates an incorrect belief that God is not truly all good or does not know what is best for us.

In my own experience, my irrational anxiety exposed this not-so-great expectation. Nothing major was wrong in my life; my husband and children were healthy and reasonably happy. I perused the areas of my life, and although circumstances were not perfect, they were pretty good. Why was I anxious? I realized I had been sailing smoothly quite a while, so I expected something to go wrong. Now some of this anxiety was understandable, since my first husband, at the age of twenty-five, died unexpectedly. In the past, life had blown up without warning. After I examined my thoughts and prayed for insight, I realized some of my anxiety stemmed from a belief that God's goodness was limited; I thought it would run out and he would want me to pay up for the good he had bestowed upon me. When I finally identified this foundational lie about God, I was able to begin to amend my thoughts with help from God's self-revelation.

He told Moses, "I will cause all my goodness to pass in front of you, and I will proclaim my name, the Lord, in your presence. I will have mercy on whom I will have mercy and I will have compassion on whom I will have compassion" (Exod. 33:19). God is infinitely merciful, good, and gracious.

Because we live in a broken world, difficult and tragic circumstances will happen. We can challenge the thoughts that accuse God's character and drive us away from him and into self-protection or anxiety. An anxious expectation of tragedy will not change or control whether good things or bad things happen. Yet, God's unlimited goodness will never change.

Jesus told a parable that reinforced the idea that God is good to all of us. A landowner hired workers five times throughout the day: early in the morning, 9:00 a.m., 12:00 p.m., 3:00 p.m., and 5:00 p.m., and he agreed to pay each worker a day's wage. When the 5:00 p.m. workers received the same pay as the others, the early morning workers complained because they expected more. The landowner reminded them that he had not been unfair; he paid the agreed-upon wage. The landowner had kept his promise to the early workers. He had been faithful and trustworthy. He was generous to the late workers. "Don't I have the right to do what I want with my own money? Or are you envious because I am generous?" (Matt. 20:15). This story reminds us that God has been good to all of us. We each have received life on this wondrous planet and the free and lavish offer of eternal life at the cost of God's only Son. Any perceived disparities in our lives diminish in light of God's truly great generosity.

Since I'm Following God, He Owes Me a Problem-Free, Pleasant Life

We expect God to give us a good life because we are his followers. We often think our obedience obligates God to reciprocate, yet God's good gift of salvation comes to us by faith. We must first come to him empty, realizing we have nothing to offer. "For it is by grace you have been saved through faith; and this not from yourselves, it is the gift of God, not by works so that no one can boast" (Eph. 2:8–9). We began a relationship with God by faith alone, and Colossians 2:6 tells us that we continue that relationship in the same way. Therefore, we continue the relationship by faith; that is, trusting God, rather than performing works for him.

This expectation that God owes us for obeying or continuing to follow him when others have quit is tenacious. This subtle but wrong thinking surfaces when difficulties arise. While working at a legal clinic through my church, a mom recounted her son's many struggles. He had bed bugs that his landlord refused to help pay to exterminate, and he lost his job. In exasperation, she exclaimed, "And he leads worship and praise in his church!" It seemed incongruent to her that these bad circumstances could happen to her son, who had done so much for God.

When expectations of how life should proceed float on the sea of disappointment, thoughts bubble to the surface. "Why is this happening to me? I am one of your children. My neighbor who does not care about you at all still has his job. He is not struggling financially." When we compare the life circumstances of followers of Jesus to those of non-followers and we come up short as we see it, we uncover our wrong expectation: if we follow God, he will always give us good circumstances.

Jeremiah expressed this perspective: "Yet I would speak with you about your justice: Why does the way of the wicked prosper?

Why do all the faithless live at ease?"(Jer. 12:1). Job also questioned this apparent unfairness. "Why do the wicked live on, growing old and increasing in power?"(Job 21:7). The Psalmist says, "For I envied the arrogant when I saw the prosperity of the wicked. They have no struggles; their bodies are healthy and strong. They are free from the burdens common to man; they are not plagued by human ills" (Ps. 73:3-5).

Elijah also may have held this expectation. Shortly after Elijah defeated Baal and his prophets, he fled in so much fear and discouragement that he prayed to die. When God asked why he was hiding in a cave, Elijah responded, "I have been very zealous for the Lord God Almighty. The Israelites have rejected your covenant, broken down your altars, and put your prophets to death with the sword. I am the only one left and now they are trying to kill me too" (1 Kgs. 19:10, 14). Elijah's answer connected his zealousness with expected favorable circumstances. He believed that if he was zealous for the Lord, his ministry to the Israelites would be successful and they would have turned back to God. Elijah's depression seems to be in part, tied to his disappointed expectation that ministry success had not been realized according to his perspective.

Doesn't life seem like this at times? It can often feel like those who are "zealous for the Lord God Almighty" have trouble and failure, while those who are not following God have a life free of struggles. While we know this is not true, our feelings of sadness and disappointment lead our minds to question the fairness and goodness of God. God graciously revised Elijah's wrong assessment of the situation. He revealed his presence in a gentle whisper, not in a powerful wind, earthquake, or fire. God further comforted Elijah not only with his presence but with the knowledge of seven thousand other Israelites who did not bow to Baal. To paraphrase God's words, if I may, "What you see is not the full picture, Elijah. I have this plan under control."

Finally, God sent Elisha, a companion and a student who would carry on the work of the Lord that Elijah had begun. Left to his own perspective, Elijah did not see the full picture. Far from God's plan spinning out of control, God had all the bases covered. Elijah's suffering reminds us that human assessments and assumptions fuel wrong expectations of life and God.

In response to a question to describe an example of a wrong expectation of God, Rosy responded with a very beautiful testimony of God's faithfulness.

> *In 2003, I met the greatest trouble I had ever encountered when my husband was diagnosed with pancreatic cancer. He died eight weeks later. During the days after the diagnosis, we both prayed deeply with each other, with our children, with our brothers and sisters in Christ, and alone. God met every need we had during those terrible days. We were unexplainably blessed by gifts of "manna" that fit the need of each day. We marveled at how God creatively brought tangible care to us, and intangible comfort. But in the end, Wayne died.*
>
> *I realized soon after the diagnosis that my husband and I were praying for opposite outcomes. Wayne prayed for a fast and painless death. I prayed for our life to return to what it was the month before the diagnosis. We prayed these conflicting requests out loud to God in the presence of each other and others. It did not take me long to realize Wayne's prayer was being answered, and mine was not. I even teased Wayne that God always gave him what he wanted. But I struggled with the reality of losing my husband.*
>
> *It kept hitting me that I had the expectation that because we were God's servants and his beloved*

*children ... and I feel ridiculous even putting this on
paper ... that he would keep us from suffering such an
untimely death. We were dedicated in our adult lives
to learning and teaching the Bible, to growing personally in prayer and fellowship with God through Christ.
We were dedicated with our prayers and money and
time to deliver the Gospel to the World. What had we
done wrong or neglected to do for the Lord that our
life together was ending this way?*

*God's kind resolution with me came the week Wayne
died as we lay in bed together. As I read the scripture
aloud to Wayne about manna, in context, I laughed
and said, "At least I'm not grumbling and saying I
want to go back to Egypt." And then I began to cry
as I realized God was showing me that I was indeed
praying that I wanted Wayne and me to go back to
our lives before the diagnosis, to Egypt. So, I was able
to say to Wayne that night, "How could I ask you to
come back to our lives here when you have one foot in
heaven?" And I meant every word.*

Whether our expectations of God appear with a case of bed
bugs or the devastating loss of a spouse, Rosy's experience reinforces
the truth, as do the lives of many other committed followers of Jesus,
that we are never promised a problem-free, "happy" life. God said
he would be with us and never leave us. And that is enough.

God Should Reveal Himself to Me

This expectation concerns God's hiddenness. We think, *If God
wants a personal relationship with me, then he should reveal himself
to me personally.* Does this sound unreasonable? If we wanted a relationship with a person, we would initiate contact with that person.
Sometimes we demand personal, unequivocally supernatural,

bowl-me-over encounters from God before we decide to follow him. I admit to having made these demands of God at a period in my life.

When my first husband died, I truly surrendered control of my life to God and received salvation. I began to experience a personal nearness to God. He revealed himself to me in many intimate ways and sometimes in seemingly supernatural experiences. I often felt his amazing and comforting presence during great grief. Throughout that period of widowhood, I was not part of a Bible-teaching church. Since I had not studied the Bible, I possessed little knowledge of God's Word. I did not know how much I did not know. Later, God orchestrated circumstances that led me to a wonderful church where everyone is highly encouraged to learn God's Word. After gaining some Bible knowledge over several years, I began to long for the early intimate "mountaintop" experiences.

I pleaded with God to reveal himself as I had experienced so clearly after my husband's death. Months passed. I kept praying but received no answer. I thought, *It is an easy thing for the God of the universe to do what I am asking. After all, he literally spoke the stars into existence. Doesn't God want personal interactions with me? This relationship feels pretty one-sided.* Before long, my prayers descended into demands and tirades with God. I then began to doubt. *Maybe he's not really there. Maybe he does not exist. Maybe Freud was right: we just want a father figure; we need a crutch.*

I asked myself why I believed in Jesus. Was it because of those initial experiences? Or, did I think biblical Christianity was true? Was the evidence of its truthfulness powerful and sufficient? Was it enough to wager my life? I reexamined foundational questions: Does God exist? What evidence supports his existence? Is he personal? Has he communicated? What evidence suggests the Bible is his communication? Were there other alleged communications from a personal deity? Was Jesus the Savior of all the world? I was honestly willing to renounce my faith and change the direction of my life away from following God.

After this period of questioning and examining the biblical evidence, as well as other philosophies and options, I concluded that biblical Christianity was convincingly the truth. Overwhelming evidence supported the fact that the Bible is God's communication to mankind. I resolved that even if I could not see, feel, or hear God, I would follow him, whether or not he ever granted me another personal experience.

The irony of that wrestling period with God was that after I recommitted and apologized to God for demanding from him, his Spirit spoke to me. When I was not expecting a response, he gently reminded me, "I have already spoken to you through the Bible. You have that now."

I immediately realized my wrong expectation: I had demanded God respond to me when he already had. After the death of my husband, he had spoken very personally and intimately to me. At that time, I desperately needed reassurance and teaching because I did not know or understand his Word. I was also not part of a community of fellow sojourners who could help me.

I remembered all God had done since that time. He brought me to a Bible-believing, Bible-teaching church where I could begin to know him deeply and continue to learn his objective and revealed Word. He *had already* revealed himself in his Word through prophets and apostles. Every human who seeks God can find him through the Bible. For the first time, I deeply realized the grace and love of God, who gave us the Bible so that each of his creatures could have direct access to him.

Not only did God make us, which he did not have to do, but he also *spoke* to us, which he did not have to do either. "In the past God spoke to our forefathers through the prophets at many times and in various ways" (Heb. 1:1).

49

Even though I now celebrate God's communication through the Bible, my quiet time can often feel dry, functional, and impersonal. I long for a personal touch, a word, sign, or sense from God. Such desires are not wrong. "As the deer longs for streams of water, so I long for you my God" (Ps. 42:1, NLT). When silence seems prolonged, doubts can creep in. We must be careful to prevent the good desire to hear a personal word from God from morphing into a wrong demand or expectation for a sign.

In *Disappointment with God,*[16] a man who wrestled with the hiddenness of God renounced him. The author, Phillip Yancey, wrote about Richard, who had dealt with many problems, both physical and emotional, in his young life. Richard expressed his last attempt to believe in God. "I felt I had to give God one last chance. I prayed as earnestly and sincerely as I knew how. I prayed, 'I don't want to tell you how to run your world, but please give me some sign that you're really there! That's all I ask.'"[17] When I read those words, my heart broke for Richard. I felt some affinity, not in his struggles, which were more than I have had to endure, but in the longing for a personal touch from God. Yet, in his prayer, I sensed an expectation. He essentially said, "I don't want to tell you how to run your world *except* in this one way: that you give me a sign you are there." Richard expected God to give him a sign, and when God did not, Richard called it quits on him. A little sign in such desperation doesn't seem too much to ask. But God has already given us a sign.

The issue of signs arose in Jesus's day as well. When the Pharisees and teachers of the law demanded a sign, Jesus refused them. He had just restored a man's sight and hearing in front of them. He said the only sign they would be given was the sign of Jonah. "For as Jonah was three days and three nights in the belly of a huge fish, so the Son of Man will be three days and three nights in the heart of the earth" (Matt. 12:40). According to Jesus, the resurrection is our sign. The resurrection attests that Jesus is who he said he was and accomplished what he said he would. To ask for a sign is acceptable; to demand a sign is not. To refuse a relationship with God because he does not meet our expectations for a personal sign is wrong and above our stature as creatures.

When we talk with God, we can pray with the expectation that the personal *and* sovereign God will determine *if, when,* and *how* he will answer or reveal himself beyond what he has already communicated. When *he knows* we need a sign, not when *we think* we need one, God will speak.

God Can't or Won't Be Able

A low expectation of God's power may harbor in our minds, and when we ignore God or do not ask him for help, it may come to light. After Job's elementary understanding of God was exposed, he humbly responded, "I know that you can do all things; no plan of yours can be thwarted" (Job 42:2). When Jesus's disciples faced an insurmountable situation, he answered them, "With man this is impossible, but with God all things are possible" (Matt. 19:26). In these two verses and many others, God reveals he is capable and powerful.

No believer in the God of the Bible would express God is incapable of anything. Our behavior, however, may betray a low expectation of God's power. The failure to pray may be one manifestation. Prayerlessness may result from many causes, but one might be a low expectation of God's ability. Abraham's wife, Sarah, possessed a low expectation of God's power. At the age of seventy-five, Sarah did not think she could get pregnant. Her belief was humanly reasonable. In our experience, seventy-five-year-old women do not become pregnant. But God, who purposed to give Abraham a descendant, asked, "Is anything too hard for the Lord?" (Gen. 18:14).

51

Might our inaction or lack of prayer demonstrate an expectation that God is not able to act? When we are physically ill or injured, do we ask God to heal? Supernatural healings do not often occur in our current human experience, much like pregnancies at seventy-five. Is this a reason not to beseech the God who spoke our frames into existence? James reminds us that one reason we might not have what we need is because we have not asked God (Jas. 4:2). In physical sickness, God is often the last person I consult. My first instinct is to research WebMD, set up a doctor's appointment, or talk to friends in the medical profession. Of course, these behaviors are not immoral. However, when we do not think to pray to God, a low expectation of God's healing power may be the cause. Yet, God is able to help us and desires us to ask, which is illustrated in a comparison of an illness event in the lives of King Asa and King Hezekiah.

Asa reformed Israel and followed God more closely than other kings of Judah. When he was afflicted with a foot disease, however, the Scriptures record, "Though his disease was severe, even in his illness he did not seek help from the Lord but only from the physicians" (2 Chron. 16:12). He died two years later. The tone of this verse suggests Asa should have asked God to heal him.

King Hezekiah also became very ill, and Isaiah informed him of his impending death. Hezekiah did ask God to spare his life, and God granted him fifteen additional years (2 Kgs. 20:1–11). Hezekiah also asked for a confirming sign after God's promise to heal him, which God granted.

What can we learn from these two accounts? God wanted both Asa and Hezekiah to ask him for healing. Asa did not, and Hezekiah did. Hezekiah was given fifteen more years of life. We don't know what God would have done had Asa asked him. Asa turned only to his physicians, and Hezekiah turned to God. God wants us to ask, and our failure to ask might reveal a low expectation of God's power or willingness.

In the New Testament, Mary and Martha asked Jesus for healing on behalf of their brother, Lazarus. "So the sisters sent word to Jesus, 'Lord, the one you love is sick'" (John 11:3). After Lazarus had been in the tomb for four days, Jesus arrived at their village, and Martha greeted him. "'Lord,' Martha said to Jesus, 'if you had been here, my brother would not have died'" (11:21). Mary expressed the same sentiment (11:32). Although the sisters confessed great faith in Jesus's ability to heal, they did not expect he could raise Lazarus from the dead. When Jesus told them Lazarus would rise, Martha affirmed he would rise at the final resurrection. Not faulting Martha and Mary, but from our vantage point, we can see they possessed a low expectation in the power of Jesus. They believed he could heal but could not awaken the dead.

If we ask God, like Hezekiah, Mary, and Martha did, we present him with the possibility of personally responding to our unique issues. We might enjoy the sense that he has seen and heard us. Finally, when we ask God for help or healing, we rightly acknowledge that he is powerful, able, and sovereignly in control over our bodies and our lives. We should always ask God for what we need, but we must not grow any expectation or demand as to how he will respond. The choice to heal or help lies entirely in the purview of the all-knowing and sovereign God.

Chapter 8:
Righteous Expectations
of God

For when you did awesome things that we did not expect (Isa. 64:3).

U p to this point, we have discussed wrong or low expectations of God that many of us commonly hold. Can we expect anything of God in a righteous, positive sense? William Carey, considered the first modern missionary, said, "Expect great things from God. Attempt great things for God."[18] Based on God's revelation, we can possess a few proper expectations.

God Will Keep His Promises

When humans make promises, we may be entitled to expect them to keep those promises. Yet, we are only warranted within the overarching and proper understanding that fallen and weak creatures will often break their promises. But God never fails. "If we are faithless, he will remain faithful for he cannot disown himself" (2 Tim. 2:13). Not only has God told us he is faithful, but we also enjoy the benefit of thousands of years of the biblical record in which God repeatedly gave and kept promises to the Jewish people. We can see his faithfulness in the promise to send a redeemer, which was fulfilled in Jesus. Without a doubt, God unfailingly keeps his promises (Heb. 10:23). The fact that God will continue to keep the promises found in his Word is a legitimate expectation. How and when those promises are fulfilled, however, is up to God.

God Will Act

Another righteous expectation is that God will act in human affairs. From Genesis to Revelation, God demonstrates that he is involved with the humans he created. He walked with Adam in the garden. He gave the gift of Eve to Adam. He provided for Adam and Eve after their rebellion. He judged wicked humanity in the flood and saved Noah and his family. He initiated a relationship with Abraham and called into being the Jewish people. Through the Jews, God set in motion a plan to reconcile humans with himself and to repair and restore the damage the separation had caused. He repeatedly sent prophets to call his people back to him. Then, from the last prophet of the Old Testament to the beginning of the New Testament, four hundred years of silence passed. To the Jewish people, it must have seemed that God was done interacting with them.

Yet, "in the fullness of time," God performed his greatest act on behalf of his creatures. He invaded human history and clothed himself as a human. In love, Jesus became one of us. He lived among the creatures, teaching and healing them. Then he died on their behalf. By dying, he accomplished a way for every sinful and rebellious human to enter a relationship with his Maker. Jesus paid for all our sins. To those who respond in faith to the Cross, Jesus gives his Spirit to dwell inside of us. The Spirit then acts in us and through us and on our behalf. And Jesus promised that he will decisively interrupt human history to return and to accomplish ultimate justice and restoration forever.

This brief metanarrative of Scripture demands the conclusion that God is indisputably involved and active with and on behalf of his creatures. "Since ancient times no one has heard, no ear has perceived, no eye has seen any God besides you, who acts on behalf of those who wait for him" (Isa. 64:4). God is indisputably involved and active with and on behalf of His creatures.

God might act in response to our asking and in ways we can see. Or, he might not. Also, there have been and will be times of silence. While

> *God is indisputably involved and active with and on behalf of His creatures.*

we can be certain that God will act, the shape and timing of his action belong to him. Our role is to pray, wait, and look with confident and eager anticipation for his activity. Waiting and watching without seeing or understanding can be difficult, yet this is what we are called to do in faith. "But as for me, I watch in hope for the Lord, I wait for God my Savior; my God will hear me" (Mic. 7:7). The wait is worth the pain, for when we see God has participated in our small lives, he communicates incomprehensible love. In this, we experience inexpressible joy that our Father has been "mindful" of us.

God Will Surprise Us

While we cannot be certain that we will accurately discern God's involvement in our affairs, when we do see his activity, he will surprise us! In Isaiah 64:1, when Isaiah asked God to act, saying, "Oh that you would rend the heavens and come down ..." he recounted that God "did awesome things that we did not expect" (Isa. 64:3). Who could expect God would part the sea and allow a million people to walk across on dry land or collapse the walls of Jericho? Who could expect that God would right the wrongs of all humanity through the death of his only Son? God is beyond our imagination. Paul acknowledges God is "able to do immeasurably more than all we ask or imagine" (Eph. 3:20). Humans cannot fully grasp what God is doing. Therefore, we wait and watch, but we also must ask God to help us to see with his eyes and his perspective.

Many times, God has surprised me with how he has answered my prayers. When I ask, I usually have some plan or expectation how God should or will answer. Although God will act, we cannot expect to know precise details. More often, he will surprise us. This was true in Old Testament examples as well.

> *The stories show that God cannot be manipulated like some good-luck charm and that he often operates outside the expected norms. In the Gideon story he confronts his people with their sin before commissioning a deliverer; in the Jephthah story he wearies of intervening, even when they persist in crying out to him and seemingly repent of their idolatry. But in the Samson story he decides to deliver even though no one asks for his help ... the stories show that deliverance often came in unexpected ways, even through flawed instruments.*[19]

If God always answered our prayers in the way we thought, we would be tempted to think more of our "powerful prayers" instead of our powerful God. When God answers our prayers beyond what we could imagine,

If God always answered our prayers in the way we thought, we would be tempted to think more of our "powerful prayers" instead of our powerful God

we are reminded he cannot be manipulated and he retains his

rightful place on the throne. And what great adventure in following such an unpredictable God!

God Will Effect Ultimate Justice

God has also promised to effect ultimate justice. God is a righteous judge, and the Bible is replete with promises that he will judge the world (Pss. 7:11; 9:8; 96:10, 13; 98:9). Acts 17:31 states, "For he has set a day when he will judge the world with justice by the man he has appointed" (see also Rom. 12:17-19; Heb. 10:27). Maintaining an expectation that God will judge can be a comfort when confronted with the horrors and devastation humans commit against each other. This can be particularly helpful when we are personally wronged, since God has commanded us not to avenge but to leave room for his just and final judgment (Rom. 12:19). Only God perceives the full scope of a person's heart and can judge justly.

Chapter 9:
Human Nature: Who Are We?

The fool doth think he is wise, but the wise man knows himself to be a fool. — *William Shakespeare*

It has already been mentioned in various contexts that a human expectation of perfection is too high. As we turn from wrong expectations of God and more fully delve into not-so-great expectations of people, the Bible's teaching about the nature of humanity is crucial.

Foundationally, humans are made in the image of God (Gen. 1:27; 9:6) and thus have intrinsic dignity and value. Yet, we have fallen from that original design (Gen. 3), and God's image in us has been twisted and marred. Specific consequences of that rebellion appear in the Genesis account. First, the wholeness of the individual was splintered, resulting in alienation inside a person. We are not comfortable in our skin; we cannot trust ourselves. In our psyche, we are broken. This brokenness manifests itself in various ways. After they sinned, Adam and Eve experienced shame for the first time and realized they were naked (Gen. 3:7). Similarly, we feel shame and the need to protect ourselves. As stated previously, this depravity includes the inability to trust our thoughts.

Next, we see a fracture in our relationship with God. Aware of their sin, Adam and Eve began to fear God and hid from him (Gen. 3:10-11). Before the rebellion, distance and separation from God had not existed. Then the first humans began to accuse, blame, and contend with one another (Gen. 3:12). Today, we too struggle with hostility and estrangement in human relationships.

Jesus, however, redeems our broken human nature. He healed each of these consequences of the fall and continues to work to repair those who accept the provision of his death as payment for rebellion and sin against God. Although we have obtained a new nature in Christ (2 Cor. 5:17; Rom. 8:9), we still sin (1 John 1:8). Our new nature will not be fully realized until we die or Christ returns.

To summarize the biblical worldview, we find the dignity in each human as a unique, beautiful creature made in God's image but also a twisted, marred, and depraved soul in rebellion against his Maker. Through Jesus, redeemed humanity has a new nature and power but continues to sin. With him, we can have "substantial healing"[20] in various areas, but the recovery of our original design will never be fully accomplished this side of eternity. The Bible's foundational truths and description of humans then inform the expectations we can legitimately hold of all people.

> *The Bible's description of humans informs the expectations we can legitimately hold of all people.*

Failure to maintain the balance of truth regarding our nature leads to not-so-great expectations. The following chapters will attempt to unpack these incorrect expectations in a variety of roles and relationships, beginning with ourselves.

Chapter 10:
Self Expectations

To be disappointed in yourself, is to have trusted in yourself. — *William R. Newell, Romans Verse by Verse*

We often face great disappointment when confronted with personal inability or failure. When our self-image or self-expectations are shattered, we are humbled. Humility naturally results when we view ourselves rightly before God as his creation, knowing we are mere creatures. Not only are we creatures, but each of us is one person among seven billion people. Our home, the earth, is one small planet in a slice of one tiny galaxy of one hundred million galaxies. In the scheme of the universe, we are microscopic, and even in our tiny domains, much of life lies outside our control.

Moreover, our time on earth is brief. "You have made my days a mere handbreadth; the span of my years is as nothing before you. Each man's life is but a breath" (Ps. 39:5). And we are sinful. All this is in contrast to God, who is utterly magnificent, powerful, eternal, and wholly good. We cannot fully comprehend the vast differences between God and His creation.

Occasionally, we glimpse some of the depth of truth about God and ourselves. Despite these insights, we tenaciously tend toward inflated views of self and create unreasonable expectations based on these views. Our wrong expectations can then lead to unnecessary self-focus and suffering.

Although Paul was often ridiculed and his authority to speak for God questioned, he instructs us through his way of handling himself in these difficulties. He sometimes responded by listing his worldly credentials such as education, Roman citizenship, family, and professional affiliation. More often, he emphasized the "credentials" of service and suffering on behalf of people. He also restrained from judging himself too closely, saying, "I care very little if I am judged by you or by any human court; indeed, I do not even judge myself. My conscience is clear, but that does not make me innocent. It is the Lord who judges me" (1 Cor. 4:3-4). Paul advocated a view of self that is not focused on adequacy or worthiness to engage in God's work, but a refusal to focus on self at all. In the words of C. S. Lewis and, more recently, Tim Keller,[21] this humble attitude has been described as "self-forgetfulness."

A few sentences later, Paul reinforced the idea that humility makes sense, that self-pride is baseless. "For who makes you different from anyone else? What do you have that you did not receive? And if you did receive it, why do you boast as though you did not?" (1 Cor. 4:7). All gifts, abilities, and opportunities are given by God. Thus, God has commanded us to "not think of yourself more highly than you ought, but rather think of yourself with sober judgment" (Rom. 12:3).

Additional voices counsel that to know ourselves accurately is essential to health. For a Christian, such knowledge does not exist apart from knowledge of God and what God has said about us in his Word. French theologian John Calvin wrote, "Our wisdom, in so far as it ought to be deemed true

To examine our thoughts in light of God's Word to discern wrong or unfounded expectations about ourselves is wholly appropriate.

and solid Wisdom, consists almost entirely of two parts: the knowledge of God and of ourselves."[22] To examine our thoughts in light of God's Word to discern wrong or unfounded expectations about ourselves is wholly appropriate.

Much of the truth about our stature in the universe, the brevity of our lives, and our sin nature comprises a negative view. But as Christians, we enjoy a new identity in Christ. We are now the beloved children of the infinite, eternal Creator. No longer do we belong to the race of Adam into which all humans are born, but God has adopted and transferred us into the family of Christ. What is true of Christ is true of us. God shouted from the heavens that Christ was his beloved Son. Can we imagine his shouting from the heavens his delight about us?

As Christians, since we know the right thing and have been given the nature and power to do it, we can begin to incorrectly expect we will always do the right thing. If we hold this expectation of self-perfection, it may be revealed particularly in areas of repeated sin. Prolonged feelings of guilt and shame might expose this expectation captured in the following thought.

I Should Have Victory over This Sin by Now

Defeat due to repeated sin can surface in areas as simple as dieting or gossip, or in deep-seated heart issues, such as envy and jealousy. When a hurtful, sarcastic remark issues out of my mouth, God reminds me how unlike Christ I truly am: "If anyone considers himself religious, and yet does not keep a tight rein on his tongue ..." (Jas. 1:26). But even more discouraging are those instances when I see the persistence and depth of my sin of self-exaltation.

My husband and I were invited to attend a short retreat with leaders in our church whom I admire and respect. After the initial feeling of excitement in being invited, my heart quickly began to bloat with all sorts of decadent thoughts. I schemed how I might reveal the invitation during a family dinner conversation, since my adult children know these leaders and would be "suitably impressed." Since we were going on retreat with some of the "rock stars" in our church, I thought they might feel privileged and happy to be our children, knowing how important their parents were. I began to worry that my words or actions would make me look stupid. Then I wondered what I could say that would shine forth the true glory of who I am so that I would finally be known and respected as I deserved. Later, I began asking why we were invited anyway...and on and on. This pathological thinking persisted throughout the retreat.

During the retreat, after listening to some recorded teachings together, the leaders began praising our good friend who had suggested a particular Bible teacher. He deflected the praise and said to my husband, "Didn't you tell me about this teacher?" My husband did not remember. Our friend's wife reminded my husband that he had been the source of discovery of the good teacher. Meanwhile, the screaming in my head went something like this: "Not this again. I discovered this particular Bible teacher and told my husband and friend about him. Am I not going to get credit again? Is my husband crazy? Does he have amnesia? Does he not remember that it was *me* who brought this good teacher to his attention?"

At this time, the Holy Spirit began to still the madness in my mind. I began to contemplate how sad and depraved it was that I wanted to steal attention and praise from my husband over the minor fact that I had stumbled upon a good Bible teacher while driving and listening to the radio. I was reminded of all the wonderful ways my husband loves and serves me. In the middle of this room of people, I silently confessed to God the insanity of trying to steal glory from my husband. I prayed, "I am sorry, God, that I cannot seem to let my husband receive praise even for such a little thing."

Then God's response popped into my head: "Yes, it doesn't make sense to steal glory from your good husband. How much less sense does it make to steal glory from *me,* who loves you more than any human and from whom you have received everything?" Although the truth hurt and humbled me, I simultaneously and deeply experienced the love of God who cares about my inward and persistent sins. Remember how small we are? And yet the infinite God disciplines each of us because we are his children (Heb. 12:6). Upon hearing God's assessment of my attempt at self-glorification, I agreed with him. Next, I thanked him that this instance of sin was also nailed on the Cross, as well as for his continuing commitment to help me change, for his involvement in my little life, and for making me feel significant through warranting his attention and loving discipline. When confronted with persistent and deep sin in ourselves, we are tempted toward desperate thinking. "We have the Holy Spirit; we have asked for help, for self-control, to not sin in this way; yet, once again, we are in the mire. Why can't we seem to change?"

When we feel such despair, questions to ask are: "Should we expect complete victory over every sin every time? Is this too great an expectation? Have we unwittingly burdened ourselves with perfection?" 1 John 1:8 states, "If we claim to be without sin, we deceive ourselves and the truth is not in us." Even with the help of the Holy Spirit, we cannot expect to always have victory over sin. However, recognition that we have too high an expectation does not negate the call to try to emulate Christ. In chapter 7 of his letter to the Romans, Paul describes the ongoing tension between our original sin nature and our new nature in Christ. To the Philippians, he acknowledged we "put no confidence in the flesh" (Phil. 3:3). These passages indicate that despite our new nature, identity, and power in Christ, we will continue to struggle with sin.

Moreover, God has an enemy in Satan. If we are aligned with God, we too are in the midst of the spiritual battle.[23] Given these truths, is it not more reasonable to expect that we will continue to sin? Shock, surprise, and disappointment merely reveal a superficial understanding of our depravity and reliance on our personal strength and power. An equal but opposite erroneous expectation is unwarranted confidence in our invulnerability to sin.

I Am Not Vulnerable to Sin in This Area

Repeated sin patterns can cause us to experience great discouragement. The Bible also warns of the danger and potential damage of thinking we have attained complete victory and are invulnerable to sin and temptation. "So if you think you are standing firm, be careful that you don't fall" (1 Cor. 10:12, NASB). Galatians 6:3 says, "If anyone thinks he is something when he is not, he deceives himself." When overconfident or deceived, we are more vulnerable, and we relax our guard. We are not cautious and may fail to install safeguards against sin and temptation.

Romans 13:14 (NASB) commands, "But put on the Lord Jesus Christ, and make no provision for the flesh in regard to its lust." One way to guard against our flesh is to ask God to give us more awareness of our weaknesses. God, who knows my inner thoughts, seemed to graciously protect me by repeatedly exposing my sin of arrogance. Many times, with an air of superiority, I have judged another person's behavior and said to myself, "What's wrong with that person? I would never do that." Often, in his mercy, God has very quickly revealed I am no different than the person I judged when I did or thought the very thing I just despised. Delving more deeply into how we can "make no provision for the flesh" (Rom.13:14, NASB), is beyond the scope of this book, but to recognize vulnerable areas seems to be a first step. In the context of self-expectation, to guard against our flesh at least means that we evaluate our thoughts concerning our power over sin and temptation. Are there areas of overconfidence where we think we "stand"?

Lest we give in to discouragement, we can replace unrealistic expectations with hope in God. When we cannot seem to stop envious or arrogant thoughts or otherwise fail to manifest the moral character of God and his Son, we can recall God's part in our struggle. He will expose "any hurtful way in me" (Ps. 139:24, NASB), and he will transform us by "the renewing of our minds" (Rom. 12:2). As we drink in God's Word, he will tailor us into the likeness of his Son.

Although God spoke these words to the nation of Israel, he promised his Spirit would *move* us to follow his decrees. Through multiple "I will" statements, God communicates that he does all the heavy lifting in helping us change.

> *I will sprinkle clean water on you and you will be clean; I will cleanse you from all your impurities and from all your idols. I will give you a new heart and put a new spirit in you; I will remove from you your heart of stone and give you a heart of flesh. And I will put my Spirit in you and move you to follow my decrees and be careful to keep my laws. (Ezek. 36:25–27)*

Finally, God somehow radiates his glory through our brokenness. "For we who are alive are always being given over to death for Jesus's sake, so that his life may be revealed in our mortal body" (2 Cor. 4:11). These promises provide us with great hope and encouragement when we are confronted with persistent sinfulness or unwarranted self-confidence trips us up. We wrestle with wrong expectations not only within ourselves but also with other people.

Chapter 11: Not So Great Expectations of People

> *But Jesus would not entrust himself to them, for he knew all people. He did not need any testimony about mankind for he knew what was in each person (John 2:24-25).*

The Bible's basic description of humans, which has been discussed in previous chapters, accurately informs us of the expectations we can have of not only ourselves but also other people. Additional verses in the Bible corroborate the fallen nature of mankind. Jeremiah 17:9 states, "The heart is deceitful above all things and beyond cure. Who can understand it?" In his letter to the Romans, Paul summarizes his argument as to the nature of mankind by stating, "For all have sinned and fall short of the glory of God" (Rom. 3:23). Despite these clear and extensive descriptions, most of us struggle with high expectations of people.

Acts chapter 3 illustrates perhaps one of the most universal expectations of other people. In this passage, Peter and John were going to the temple at the time of afternoon prayer when they came upon a beggar crippled from birth. The beggar asked Peter and John for money, whereupon the apostles *looked straight* at him and commanded the man to look back at them. "So the man gave them his attention, expecting to get something from them" (Acts 3:5). If anyone noticed or *looked* at the man, he likely received a coin. Yet, Peter quickly disappointed the man's expectation, saying, "Silver or gold I do not have, but what I have I give you. In the name of Jesus Christ of Nazareth, walk" (3:6). This brief encounter captures a snapshot of our hearts. Like the beggar, we generally look to people "expecting to get something from them."

God designed us in his image, and he is relational. From eternity, God existed in a community of persons, the Trinity, who love each other. We too were built for relationship. Before the creation of Eve, God declared that Adam's isolation was not good. Our desire and need to relate with other humans is intrinsic to our design and thus essential to a life of wholeness and health.

Yet, our greatest source of pain often results from relationships. The rebellion of mankind explains much of the brokenness we experience. None of our human relationships can completely or perfectly meet our needs. One way in which we sin against each other and cause relational discord is through not-so-great expectations. We look to other humans to *receive* from them, expecting them to provide more than they are able. We demand that people fulfill our needs and desires, forgetting that God has promised to meet our needs (Phil. 4:19). Like the account of the beggar in Acts, God often works through other people to meet our needs and sometimes gives us more than we ask. The beggar's expectation for money was disappointed, but through Peter and John, God healed his lameness.

When we experience pain or conflict with other marred image-bearers of God, part of the problem may involve unspoken and unwarranted expectations. These arise in the everyday affairs of life. We expect polite customer service (the customer is always right) and friendly and thoughtful neighbors. We may have high expectations while driving, which, when disappointed, could escalate into road rage. We commonly expect gratitude if we give gifts or perform a service for someone else.

Are these reasonable expectations? Should we demand others live up to our standards as to how they should act in particular situations? What can we properly expect of people? In John 2:24-25, Jesus states that he would not entrust himself to people because "he knew" them and "he knew what was in each person." What does this text indicate?

Some commentators suggest Jesus would not entrust himself to the onlookers who superficially believed in him "because of the signs." Others propose this indictment applies to all mankind because we are rebellious and fallen. Still, others comment that John was subtly ascribing deity to Jesus since the Jewish people recognized that God always knew the hearts of all people. These options are not mutually exclusive. The broad language and the repetition supports the conclusions that John may have intended to convey all those thoughts. Jesus did possess divine knowledge of the sinful hearts of humans. He was not going to entrust himself to those who believed in him only because of the signs nor to anyone because, as the text repeats, he knew what was in each person.

But the staggering thought is that although Jesus would not entrust himself to people, He would die for them.

Through His life, Jesus provides a model for us in relationships. He would not entrust himself to people but he died for them. Therefore, we too should not entrust ourselves to people. To expect too much from others is a form of entrusting ourselves to them. If we depend on others to fulfill our needs, we have delivered ourselves into the hands of other fallen humans. Emotions, such as extreme disappointment in other people, may expose the reality that we have so entrusted ourselves.

In whom should we place our trust? Peter, in the context of suffering, encouraged his readers to "entrust themselves" to a faithful Creator. "So if you are suffering in a manner that pleases God, keep on doing what is right, and trust your lives to the God who created you, for he will never fail you" (1 Pet. 4:19, NLT). According to Peter and Jesus, we should entrust ourselves to God. But the staggering thought is that although Jesus would not entrust himself to people, He would die for them.

Again, Jesus would *die* for us even though he would not *entrust* himself to us. This then is the model for our relationships with others as well. God has called us to love one another. "This is how we know what love is: Jesus Christ laid down his life for us. And we ought to lay down our lives for our brothers and sisters" (1 John 3:16). Of course, to love others, it is not necessary that we physically die. Only the perfect Christ qualifies to die for another, and this he has already accomplished. To love others involves denying ourselves, dying to ourselves through elevating the needs of others above our own. One way we can lay down our lives is to surrender our not-so-great expectations of one another. We do not look to get something from them or entrust ourselves to them, yet like Jesus, we must be willing to die to ourselves for them.

In our relationships, to expect little and sacrifice much seems like an impossibly high standard. But isn't Christ our perfect model to imitate? In all areas, we look to Jesus to inform us about how to live and love. Even as we know we will not be able to achieve the perfection of Jesus, he corrects our thinking, specifically our wrong expectations, so we know at what to aim and what our part in relationships should look like. Jesus also provides the model for where to draw the strength and power to attempt self-sacrifice.

Like Jesus, we primarily depend on God for our relational needs. In every pain and disappointment from people, we turn our minds and hearts to God and his love for us. If we entrust ourselves and depend more on God for our relational needs, we will be strengthened to love more like Jesus, and we will try to give to others without looking to receive or expecting anything from them. In the next chapter, we will specifically explore the nature of expectations in our relationships with friends.

Chapter 12:
Not So Great Expectations
of Friends

One who loves a pure heart and who speaks with grace will have the king for a friend (Prov. 22:11).

Should we have different expectations of people we consider friends? Biblical examples would suggest not. Job's friends failed him. "My relatives have gone away; my friends have forgotten me" (Job 19:14). Also, David's suffering was heightened due to the abandonment of friends, which he mentions many times in the Psalms. "My friends and companions avoid me because of my wounds; my neighbors stay far away" (Ps. 38:11). "Even my close friend, someone I trusted, one who shared my bread has turned against me" (Ps. 41:9). "If an enemy were insulting me, I could endure it; if a foe were raising himself against me, I could hide from him. But it is you, a man like myself, my companion, my close friend with whom I once enjoyed sweet fellowship as we walked with the throng at the house of God" (Ps. 55:12-14). Almost all of the friends of Jesus either betrayed him, denied him, or left him alone in the garden through his trial and upon the cross. Paul experienced pain when at a time of great need, his friends abandoned him. "At my

73

first defense, no one came to my support, but everyone deserted me" (2 Tim. 4:16).

Relationships with friends are perhaps the most challenging area in which to surrender expectations, particularly because we tend to expect more from friends than acquaintances. Sometimes the closest relationships yield the greatest demands. Expectations build from shared experiences and recurrent patterns of relating. Is it okay if we expect our friends to act a certain way? Most friendships contain implied and sometimes explicit agreements regarding the relationship between those involved, but unanticipated and unspoken expectations arise and create the potential for unnecessary conflict and even the loss of the friendship. In most friendships, we will grow expectations of our friends, who will disappoint those expectations. Additionally, our friends will develop expectations of us that we will disappoint. Friends can disappoint our expectations either by commission or omission. They may commit hurtful acts against us, such as gossip or theft.

More often, a friend omits doing what we think they should do. "You did not return my call or text." "You should have called when I was sick." "You should have come when I was injured." "You did not call for two weeks after my husband left." "You did not help when the storm wrecked my house." "You did not reach out to me when my world was falling apart." "You did not notice my pain." We feel certain that our friends should have performed a particular course of action. In friendships, real or perceived failures abound and are as unlimited and varied as people and situations. These failures can be summarized in the following expectation.

You Failed to Love Me in the Way I Want to Be Loved

A small but common disappointed expectation concerns the obligation to return communications: phone calls, texts, or emails.

One time, after a friend had not responded to a text, I began to question the legitimacy of my expectation. I wondered, *Does my text create an obligation for the recipient to reply? Is there an unwritten, unspoken but agreed code of conduct in friendships?* When I was processing these thoughts, I raised the issue with a friend. I suggested returning calls or texts was a nice thing to do but not an unbreakable duty or obligation of friendship. My friend reacted strongly and replied, "Of course you should call a friend back. That's the right thing to do."

I noticed the elevated emotion in her voice but continued my thoughts aloud. "Since we look to God as our guide to relationships, Scripture is not specifically clear that a return text is required." I smiled, hoping to lighten the tension and joked, "At least there was no direct command, 'Thou shall return all communications with people.' Maybe," I continued, "responding to communication falls under the blanket command to be kind to one another. It does seem to be kind or courteous." Mutual communication is the foundation of any relationship. But must it be immediate as our modern technological society encourages? Is there no room for delay or forgetfulness? I admitted to my friend the many occasions when I failed to return friends' communications. "Have you ever failed?" I asked. We further explored and questioned our expectations. Even if we decided it is unkind to fail to respond to a text or call, do we expect perfection? We must be aware of and prevent unwarranted expectations of unfailing kindness in our relationships.

The most reasonable expectation in friendships is that friends will often fail to do what we want them to do. *We* will often fail. Friends will neglect even what they believe they *should* do in relationships. People will disappoint each other in relatively small issues such as a failure to return communications, as well as in significant ways such as betrayal and abandonment, as we see in the situations of Job, David, Jesus, and Paul. Friendships, and all relationships, are paradoxically risky. We could get hurt. We *will* be hurt. Yet, without relationships, we are incomplete and unfulfilled. A low expectation of friends is legitimate because it is based on the overarching reality of the human condition.

How should we respond to our friend's failures, whether real or perceived? The answer, the good news to such a sad state of affairs, is that we can look to God and not to people for what only God can provide. These truths, our innate need for relationship and the unavoidable failure of humans, drive us to the only perfect person, to the only one who made it blood-stained clear that he desires a close and intimate relationship with us, to God, who has done everything necessary in the death of his only Son to offer and become our only perfect and unfailing friend. Only Jesus was abandoned by God, and only at the Cross. "My God, My God, why have you forsaken me?"(Matt. 27:46; Mark 15:34). Because of Jesus, God will never forsake us. Even though friends will fail us, we will never be abandoned by God.

David, Jesus, and Paul modeled this dependence on God. In the Psalms, David pours out his hurts, fears, angers, all his emotions to God. He often wrestles with God in his confusion over the actions of both friends and enemies, but he always ends these moments with cries for help (Ps. 38:22) and expressions of trust and hope in God (55:22-23). Similarly, Jesus called to mind God's sustaining presence immediately after predicting the disciples' abandonment: "But a time is coming, and has come, when you will be scattered, each to his own home. You will leave me all alone. Yet I am not alone, for my Father is with me" (John 16:32). Paul imitated the example of Jesus with his friends. In 2 Timothy, when Paul's

> *We lower expectations of other humans and consequently can enjoy close friendships as we rest in our perfect friendship with God.*

friends deserted him, he offered them forgiveness: "May it not be held against them" (4:16). How could he do this? The next verse explains. "But the Lord stood at my side and gave me strength so that through me the message might be fully proclaimed and all the Gentiles might hear it" (4:17). Paul entrusted himself to God. He claimed the truth that God was with him, by his side, giving him strength. Paul also focused on his mission from God more than his relational hurt. The examples of David, Jesus, and Paul model God-oriented and gracious principles for relationships.

Disappointed expectations of friends move us to place the weight of our relationships onto God through Jesus. They encourage a more truthful understanding of ourselves and others. We lower our expectations of other humans and consequently can enjoy close friendships as we learn to extend grace and forebear while we rest in our perfect friendship with God.

To entrust ourselves to God includes trying to learn from him in the ways in which we relate to others, including our friends. Looking to or depending on God does not mean that we retreat from relationships. Rather, God calls us to love and has designed us for relationship with him and others.

Jesus taught three very practical steps to extend grace to others and relate well when faced with inevitable conflicts or not-so-great expectations. In Matthew 7:5, Jesus declares the order of judging wrongs committed, saying, "First take the plank out of your own eye." When a friend has disappointed us, we should begin to resolve our hurt by examining ourselves including our expectations. Ask yourself, "Are my expectations too high? Am I seeking perfection in a fallen human being? Has this person's relationship become too important?" Look through the disappointment to discern whether God is revealing an idol or growing your character and increasing your dependence on him. Look *first* at what is wrong inside yourself.

Next, in Matthew 7:7-11, Jesus prescribes that we should keep asking God, seeking God, and knocking on His door to have him meet our needs. Our relational needs can appear in many forms: to be noticed or appreciated, comforted, or loved. We ask God for what we think we relationally need. Of course, his assessment of what we need might be different than our own, and it is authoritative.

Finally, Jesus commands us to treat others the way we want to be treated (7:12). How do we want to be treated? We want forgiveness and forbearance. We want the benefit of the doubt that our failures were not malicious or intended to be hurtful. We want second chances.

What we should *not* do is treat our friends badly, punish them, or get revenge for their failures. We should not make demands for certain behaviors or apologies. We should not withdraw, give our friends the silent treatment, or avoid them. We should not make excuses or rationalize our wrong responses to their "failures." We should count the cost of the potential loneliness and isolation that will come from losing friendships if we hold onto our demands and our expectations. In most instances, we should simply forebear with one another and talk honestly with God.

In limited circumstances, such as in long-term relationships with repeated conflict, we may need to communicate our hurts with friends. In Neil Anderson's book *Victory over the Darkness,*[24] he sets forth three ways to handle emotions. We can suppress, indiscriminately express, or acknowledge them. Of course, suppressing our emotions is not helpful. Anderson suggests indiscriminate expression of our emotions should only be done with God. David and other authors of the Psalms perhaps illustrate full and complete expression of emotions to God. He can handle this. Acknowledging emotions, Anderson suggests, is a healthy practice before God and people. However, because we cannot trust ourselves, we need to carefully acknowledge our emotions with people after much soul-searching with God. We should express our disappointments with friends when God persuades us that to do so is for their good or necessary for the health of our friendship, not for us to get something from them. Honest and vulnerable conversations contribute to relational closeness, unity, and mutual respect. Many helpful books have been written that teach gracious communication.[25] Even a basic discussion is well beyond the scope of this book or my understanding or ability, but I will offer a few basic thoughts. Returning to the example of texts, emails, or phone calls, one friend could express hurt by the lack of response, using "I felt" language instead of "you did/did not or should have" accusations. In order to understand what happened in a situation or a friend's perspective on responding to communication, we can gently ask the other friend their thoughts. Friends can certainly agree to try to meet each other's desires and expectations after they are explicitly communicated to each other.

But the majority of the time, we hang the weight of our relationships on God and look to him to meet our relational needs. We sincerely seek God, our good Father and unfailing Friend. When we ask for and experience his provision for our relational needs, we will develop "emotional wealth—a sense of being loved so deeply that when someone wrongs us we can afford to be generous, able to forgive."[26] In Isaiah 49:23, the sovereign Lord promises, "Those who hope in me will not be disappointed."

Some may think this perception is too negative, and if we stopped only at this conclusion, we would have no hope for enjoyable and lasting relationships. However, the opposite is true. Friendships with others are great blessings from God and the following examples demonstrate that perhaps God-oriented friendships provide the greatest chance for success. We can observe good and godly friendships in the Bible. One such example is the friendship of David and Jonathan, the son of King Saul. Jonathan surrendered his right to his father's throne and saved David's life, illustrating self-sacrificial love (1 Sam. 18-20). Jonathan entrusted himself to God and his plan for David to become the next king. Through friends, like Jonathan, we will receive many of God's good gifts.

In my opinion, nothing is sweeter than to experience God meeting my needs in various ways, sometimes directly but often through his people. In spring of the year when my oldest daughter was making plans to attend college in August, I began to feel sadness for her departure and the change in our family dynamic. I would no longer have all my children in the same house. I expressed this sadness to friends in my women's Bible study and often asked for prayer. In late July, while at my son's baseball game, I mentioned my sorrow to another woman, an acquaintance named Mary, who attended our church. Then, a month later, when the dreaded day in August arrived, I was driving home alone, sobbing after moving my daughter into her college living quarters. My husband did not share these emotions to the same extent, so I felt alone. I prayed all the way home. "God, I feel so sad and alone. Is my sadness out of proportion? I had talked about this with my friends and asked for prayer for months, and in addition to my sadness, my pain feels unnoticed and forgotten."

Hearing my thoughts in prayer revealed to me an expectation that my close friends in the Bible study would remember and call. This expectation was disappointed. The extent of my grief also exposed an idol in my life concerning my children. Yet, God graciously heard my prayer. I arrived home and walked in the door to the phone ringing. The baseball mom, Mary, with whom I had no contact since our conversation a month previously, was on the phone. She said, "I was in my hammock praying when God brought you to my mind, and I remembered that your daughter was moving out soon. I wanted to call and ask how you were doing." I again started to cry, but this time, tears of joy flowed, for my Father God had noticed me and moved someone to call. Although this event occurred many years ago, the memory of how God blessed me and met my need through Mary continues to strengthen my faith and provides emotional wealth from which I can draw in times of relational hurt with friends.

Paul experienced God's blessing through people as well. "And they exceeded our expectations: They gave themselves first of all to the Lord, and then by the will of God also to us" (2 Cor. 8:5). The Corinthian people responded to God first in financial generosity, which flowed into blessing Paul. Paul's friends in Ephesus wept when they realized they would not see him again, demonstrating closeness and deep love (Acts 20:37–38). While under arrest and on his way to stand trial in Rome, his friends in Sidon ministered to his needs (Acts 27:3).

Similarly, in my life, Mary responded to God's prompting, which resulted in a blessing to me from God. If each of us lives vertically oriented to God, seeking to have God meet our needs and simultaneously seeking for God to use us to bless others, we will experience great relational blessings from God through friends like Mary. We will also experience the incredible privilege of being a blessing to our friends. These principles apply to all our friendships, but a few differences exist with our Christian friends and will be addressed in the next chapter.

Chapter 13:
Friendships in Church

Above all, love each other deeply, because love covers over a multitude of sins (1 Pet. 4:8).

Much of what has been written concerning expectations of friends applies to fellow Christians. Whether our friends are Christians or not, our responsibility to imitate Jesus in all our relationships remains the same. However, our Christian friends are also our spiritual family, which is the Bible's most-often-used metaphor for the church of Jesus Christ. Moreover, to love others like Christ loved as demonstrated on the Cross is the calling of every Christian. "This is how we know what love is: Jesus Christ laid down his life for us. And we ought to lay down our lives for our brothers" (1 John 3:16). So in the situation of Christian friendships, we are not only family, but both sides of the friendship possess the same objective. Because we know the higher standards of behavior that Christ calls us to in the family of Christ, we may develop greater expectations of our brothers and sisters than those we have concerning our friends who do not follow Christ. These expectations may be too high, unfair, or unrealistic. For example, we may expect our Christian friends to always and perfectly meet our needs.

Since Christians Know the Lord and the Bible, They Will Meet My Needs

The Bible unpacks the broad command to love one another. Over fifty verses direct how we should treat fellow believers, including to encourage, accept, admonish, serve, forebear, and comfort one another. We are commanded to be devoted, hospitable, submissive, and kind to each other. Negatively, we are told not to complain, judge, or lie to one another. Some Christians use these verses as the basis for their high expectations of others in the church. However, it is important to acknowledge that these imperatives concerning our brothers and sisters are from God. We owe obedience of the commands first to him. We love our brothers and sisters primarily as a response to God's love and command. Our fellow Christians are third-party beneficiaries of our obligation to God.

> *Our fellow Christians are third-party beneficiaries of our obligation to God*

When we fall short of these standards, we first offend God. A derivative consequence results in harm to our brothers and sisters. To hold other Christians to perfectly keep these commands is unrealistic, for by doing so, we are looking for fallen humans to meet our relational needs. As has been said before, such expectations hint at idolatry.

In friendships with other Christians, we have the added concern for unity. We must consider the serious potential that we might destroy the unity of God's family and malign the character of God when the watching world sees no better relationships among Christians. But the good news with our Christian friendships is that not only do we share the same mission to love like Jesus, we all have the same standards in God's Word at which to aim. In God's Word, we have clear direction for our part in relationships.

We also possess the powerful resource of the indwelling of the Holy Spirit. When we disappoint our Christian friends or they disappoint us, we can pray and trust the Holy Spirit will expose any hurtful way or necessary change in our hearts, as well as expose and work whatever change is needed in the hearts of our Christian friends. Early in our marriage, I realized the Holy Spirit was the one who would convict us and help us change. I had talked to my husband about an issue but did not want to nag (Prov. 21:9, 19, HCSB), so I began to pray that the Holy Spirit would convict my husband (unknown to him) about the issue in which I thought he should change. After about a week, my husband expressed to me that he felt such conviction. I thought I had stumbled on the way to make my husband conform to my ideas of how he should act, which was really a veiled attempt to manipulate another human.

The next time I prayed in this way for my husband, it did not "work." When I continued praying, God convicted me that the problem was mine, not my husband's, and I needed to change. Other times, God answered that my timing was not his timing in working change in my husband. Praying for our fellow Christians and asking on their behalf for God to help them change is a gracious work for one another. Paul's prayer at the end of Hebrews is a beautiful example of this. He prays, "May the God of peace ... work in us what is pleasing to him" (13:20-21). Paul's prayer was for himself and others, as he asked that God would work what was pleasing to him, not what was pleasing to Paul. His prayer for others was God-focused. Therefore, our prayers for others should similarly be less about the correction we think another person needs or their offense against us and more about God working in them—what he knows they need and what pleases him. Then we must wait for God's Spirit to operate on each of us, for change in ourselves or others is generally a slow process that involves much patience and forbearance.

What legitimate expectations can we have of our Christian friends? Although they possess the commands of God and desire to obey, they will fail to achieve these standards, and we will fail at this too. We should not be surprised when a Christian does not serve when help seems needed or when encouragement is absent in times of discouragement. We should not be surprised by this, nor should we expect our believing friends will always respond to God's call to love; even if they respond, we should not expect that they will perform perfectly. We must ask ourselves, "How many times have I ignored the prompting of the Holy Spirit to call or reach out or otherwise love someone?" Although we are new creatures, we continue to live in the sinful world with a sinful nature that is not fully destroyed. A correct expectation then is that sometimes Christians will act like Christ and other times they will not. But according to the promise of God, he will meet our needs and often will do so through other Christians. To experience God meeting our needs through our brothers and sisters is joyful; to experience the joy of being God's instrument of His love toward other Christians is even better. We can pray regularly to hear from the Lord as to how and who he wants us to serve. We can pray for his help to follow through on such promptings by the Spirit.

Much hope results from this kind of living; our choices are independent of others. There is great freedom in looking to God alone. When others disappoint us, we can choose to forebear and forgive; we can choose patience. "A man's wisdom gives him patience; it is to his glory to overlook an offense" (Prov. 19:11). Ajieth Fernando wrote, "Christians who approach life in this way will be happy people. Other people may not respond to their actions in the way they hoped. But this does not leave believers disillusioned and angry—a condition that describes many people in humanitarian

85

service. When we have loved, we have been successful. God has seen and he will reward." [27] As far as God is concerned, if we have tried to love others, even if feebly, he is pleased. Especially with our Christian friends, we need the overflow of grace, forgiveness, and forbearance from God. We need the power of God to live as honorably and sacrificially as our Savior, Jesus Christ. Once again, Jesus is the ideal standard for our friendships in the church: like Christ, we die to self for the good of others but entrust ourselves to God alone. In our Christian friendships, if we only get this right half of the time, someone is acting like Jesus! There is reason to hope for close and healthy relationships with Christian friends. However, specific relationships in the church may give rise to unique expectations.

Discipleship Relationships

Some friendships in the church begin with a common goal and explicit purpose, such as discipleship. Jesus commanded us to make disciples, and his life demonstrated disciple-making with a small group of men. Through discipleship, his objective was to help them grow in their relationship with God and prepare them for their mission. Paul also embraced discipleship and instructed Timothy, his disciple, to continue this ministry (2 Tim. 2:2).

In response to these commands and examples, many Christians enter into Christ-centered friendships or discipleship relationships with the same goal: to help nurture one another's relationship with and service to God. They may expressly commit to regular meeting times for Bible study and prayer. At the beginning of these relationships, good communication may inhibit future misunderstandings. However, in the context of these relationships, other expectations may arise that go beyond what is agreed. Statements such as "You are not meeting my need in this area," "You are not giving me enough time," or "I wish it was someone else helping me," may reveal a dependence on a disciple instead of on God. The one being mentored may grow an idol of the mentor, looking to them to provide everything they need. Perhaps a person may believe they are owed this type of commitment; however, we are not owed a discipleship relationship. We can ask others to disciple us, but we must never demand this.

In discipleship, not-so-great expectations can occur with both parties. The mentor must be careful not to call disciples to follow human ideas or add standards of behavior not found in God's Word; rather, the mentor must point them to live unto God and his commands and principles. Because such relationships usually result in deep friendships and we often expect more of our closest friends, discipleship relationships, in particular, may need to be closely monitored for unrealistic expectations.

These relationships, however, also provide an ideal context to specifically address wrong expectations. When mentoring another person toward maturity in Christ, wrong expectations might be revealed as a source of continuing relational conflict. In *Organic Discipleship,* authors McCallum and Lowery describe people engaged in "high expectation relating" as "hard to please" or "high maintenance." The authors explain, "They seem to feel they deserve a certain standard of treatment from others. Properly understood, these expectations are really love-demands that make a person a love-taker rather than a love-giver."[28] The authors suggest that confronting high expectations is essential to help a person's spiritual growth. Maturity involves becoming like Christ, the ultimate Giver of love.

If someone is willing to commit to a relationship for mutual growth in Christ-likeness, such willingness is an act of love toward us and a great blessing from God. A reasonable expectation in discipleship is that the relationship will often be messy and challenging.

No one will disciple perfectly, but God will grow both individuals through the relationship and their commitment to follow him.

Relationships with Leaders

Expectations of other Christians may also occur in the context of relationships with leaders. In Titus 1 and 1 Timothy 3, the Bible lists qualifications for leaders that overwhelmingly concern character. 1 Peter 5 instructs that leaders should serve willingly, eagerly, and with humility. These high standards express God's ideals for servant leadership. No human will achieve perfection in these areas, but those charged with appointing leaders need to consider these biblical qualities. Still, followers need to be very careful not to grow unrealistic expectations of leaders.

The Leaders Have Failed Me or This Group by …

Many various endings to this sentence are possible. We can unwittingly begin to require moral perfection of leaders, or we may demand they make specific strategic decisions following our opinions. When conflict arises between us and anyone in authority, we should check our expectations of them. As in friendships, leaders are first accountable to God for their leadership (Heb. 13:17). A leader's accountability to God does not mean that we should not evaluate leaders for heresy or ongoing and serious moral failures. We should not carelessly follow leaders; instead, we can and should respectfully ask questions, bring up concerns, and interact with strategic decisions as God's Spirit leads. Most leaders would welcome such questions because they demonstrate investment and concern for the group. We also need to be willing to come alongside our leaders as fellow sinners in the struggle for Christ-like maturity.

Ideally, other structures of authority are in place to oversee leaders. We can remind ourselves of the truth that "there is no authority except which God has established" (Rom. 13:1). Therefore, we can trust that God directs leaders. Our responsibility is primarily to obey, submit, and remember them, which includes praying for them (Heb. 13:7, 17). God has called us to help carry their burden so their work can be a joy. A good question to ask might be, "Am I a joy to my leader, or do I demand too much from them?"

Due to high expectations, relationships with friends, mentors, and leaders in the church seem particularly vulnerable to destruction, and they are likely more susceptible to attacks from God's enemy, Satan. For when we achieve success in these relationships, from God's perspective, we contribute to the unity of God's church, which is a powerful light in a dark world. If we practice the "one another" verses and resolve relational conflicts with our church family according to Matthew 7, unity results and we experience much peace and joy in our relationships. When we entrust ourselves only to God while laying down our lives for others, like Jesus did, God is glorified, and others will be attracted to such other-worldly relationships.

This chapter has addressed the distinct expectations of Christians by other Christians. In the next chapter, we will briefly consider the expectations of Christians by those outside the church.

Chapter 14:
Not So Great Expectations of Christians

> *Therefore, as we have opportunity, let us do good to all people (Gal. 6:10).*

N ot only do Christians unreasonably expect certain conduct from other Christians, many outside the church are disappointed in their observations of Christians.

Christians Shouldn't Act Like That

People who do not follow Christ or know God's Word often have preconceived ideas or misconceptions about Christians. Someone's disappointed expectations concerning a Christian's behavior can often be traced to a misunderstanding of the core of Christianity. Many believe that a Christian is a person who tries to engage in high moral conduct in order to be acceptable to God. Therefore, when a Christian acts immorally, those who hold this understanding judge the Christian's failure to live by a moral standard and are disappointed. In the introduction of this book, examples were cited, such as a youth pastor arrested for child molestation and the unrighteous anger of Christians at a military funeral. Mean-spirited slander and gossip at a women's Bible study or the sins of omission when we look the other way after being confronted by an easily-met need are all ways in which we do not reflect God.

Christians, as discussed, are called to the highest standards of morality, to love all the way to the cross. Yet, we remain sinful creatures; although forgiven and redeemed, we are not perfect. Until Christ returns, we live in the tension between our identity as God's people and the condition of our sinful selves. To expect moral perfection is to hold a misunderstanding of Christianity.

The foundational belief of Christianity is that God freely offers the gift of a restored relationship with him through the payment for our sins by Jesus Christ. We live in relationship with God by the power of the Holy Spirit. True godly moral living largely comes as a *result* of that relationship and an ongoing daily choice to follow Jesus or not. We should freely admit with sadness that we often do not choose Jesus's way. At any moment, some followers accurately reflect Jesus, while others do not represent him well. Such renewal and transformation is a lifelong process and is not always on a smooth or even an upward trajectory. To hold Christians to the perfect example of Christ is expecting too much of them.

We can review Christian history or other's actions in light of God's Word and deplore certain behavior as unlike Christ. When appropriate, we should agree with that assessment of others. But with humility, we should also realize that we do not know the pressures of the choices of people in their time of history and leave the ultimate judgment in the hands of God. We all can remember yesterday when, at many points throughout the day, we ourselves did not act like Christ. May we thank God for his mercy and grow in humility and gratitude for his rescue.

As Christians, we need to be aware of what our culture perceives about us because, whether we like it or not, we are representatives of Jesus. We should listen and prayerfully discern before God the critiques that are truly not reflective of him. When the criticisms are correct and we are not living according to God's standards, we should seek God's help and ask him for the power to change in response. However, we should not look primarily to our culture or its changing views for our choices and behavior. The preoccupying question for the Christian is, what does God expect of us?

What Does God Expect of Us?

In this chapter, which examines the expectations of Christians from people outside of the church, it seems fitting to ask this more important question: what does God expect of us? Much of our life concerns this question in our relationship with God. We may ask him, "What do you want me to do in this particular time or situation?" Generally, a few answers can universally be applied to all humans for all time.

First and foremost, God desires but does not demand his creatures to enter into a relationship with him. However, he does expect and require this relationship to begin and continue on his terms, through his Son, Jesus. Why can God insist on his terms? A teacher told the following story to illustrate this truth. A man climbed a ladder, broke a second-story window, and entered another man's house. The listeners were asked what the homeowner should be permitted to do when confronted. The unanimous response held that the homeowner would be justified to shoot and kill the intruder. When asked why the intruder could not come into the man's house any way he wanted, the analogy was clear. We are entering God's presence—his house, so to speak. God has the right and supreme authority to tell us we can only enter his presence through Jesus. "I am the way and the truth and the life. No one comes to the Father except through me" (John 14:6). "I am the door; if anyone enters through Me, he will be saved" (John 10:9, NASB).

Micah the prophet answers this question regarding God's expectations for Israel. "He has shown you, O man, what is good. And what does the Lord require of you? To act justly and to love mercy and to walk humbly with your God" (6:8). God's first desire is that we receive his offer of a relationship in the way that God prescribes, namely through his Son's death on the Cross, that we love him, and that we humbly journey through life with him. As we walk and dwell in the presence of God, who personifies mercy and justice, while beholding him continually, we will hopefully choose mercy and justice and do good more often, thus better representing him. Paul writes, "Therefore, as we have opportunity, do good to all people, especially to those who belong to the family of believers" (Gal. 6:10). Yet, when we fail, because of his lovingkindness, God can and does use our failures to nevertheless draw people to himself. Others may begin to understand that moral perfection is not the basis of our relationship with God, and our failure may accentuate that we all need Jesus, the Savior.

In all of our relationships, mercy is needed, especially with our friends and family. We will now turn the discussion to not-so-great expectations in family relationships, beginning with marriage.

Chapter 15: Expectations in Marriage

> *"You are a sinner, your spouse is a sinner and you live in a sinful world."* — Paul Tripp, *What Did You Expect?*

Marriage provides rich soil in which to grow expectations. Much has been written regarding expectations in marriage. One book on marriage is aptly entitled *What Did You Expect?* Early in the book, the author, Paul Tripp, succinctly diagnoses the reasons for disappointed expectations in marriage: "You are a sinner, your spouse is a sinner and you live in a sinful world." [29] Tripp suggests that if we accept these truths, we can begin to "redeem the realities of marriage." One of these realities is that not-so-great expectations will be disappointed. Many resources can help with disappointed marital expectations; in this book, my goal is to help you uncover and recognize when personal expectations are involved in marital conflict. To that end, we will discuss two wide-ranging but common expectations that may wound a marriage.

My Spouse Will Make Me Completely Fulfilled or Happy

"You complete me." These famous romantic words were spoken by the title character in the movie *Jerry Maguire*. [30] To criticize a

fictional movie line in a serious book on expectations may seem
unnecessary, yet many expectations originate with the media, even
when we know we are watching a work of fiction. Many of us enter
marriage with that exact idea that a spouse will fill what we lack;
always meet our needs; and provide all the companionship, happiness, help, security, significance, and sex we desire. We would not
usually admit or express such high expectations, and we might not
even know they are lurking in our thoughts. We might only discover we had such an expectation after we have experienced pro-
found marital disappointment. How might this be manifested? One
humorous and often-cited difference in needs is when a wife wants
to talk, express her feelings, and verbally process, while her husband feels impatient to fix the problem. The wife may find she is
better able to meet her need or desire for long conversations about
her feelings with a girlfriend. Or, the husband may try to develop
longer listening skills without trying to fix the underlying issue.
Until the different expectations are recognized, much hurt and conflict between a husband and a wife may erupt.

A marriage built on the high expectation that a spouse will meet
all our needs establishes a flimsy foundation. When we hold this
wrong expectation, we are positioning a human as an idol, putting
that human in a place where only God belongs. As mentioned
before, making an idol of another person will destroy a relationship
through unreasonable pressure, since a human is not able to bear
the weight of God's space. In a previous example from the Bible, the
king of Israel tore his clothes in great distress when the king of Aram

*God's purpose for marriage goes beyond
simply meeting relational needs to creating a
rich environment for the cultivation of
the character of Christ*

asked him to heal his commander, Naaman (2 Kgs. 5:6-8). The king of Israel felt great pressure to heal, something he was not able to do. In marriage, neither spouse is equipped to always meet the other's needs.

Many single adults may labor under this misunderstanding and so greatly desire a spouse, thinking their needs will be fully met through marriage. The longing for companionship or a partner in life is not wrong, but a fallen human cannot and will not meet all our relational needs. Even when we try to meet the needs of another, we do so imperfectly. Only God can ultimately provide for us adequately and perfectly. He promises to meet our needs, whether we are single or married. He will meet our needs through other people or in ways we cannot anticipate, and he can and often will meet these needs through a spouse. However, to expect a marriage partner to always meet our needs, especially in specific ways, sets up an unrealistic expectation that will destroy our marriage. God's purpose for marriage goes beyond simply meeting relational needs to creating a rich environment for the cultivation of the character of Christ.

Such sanctification or growth in Christ-like character will happen in all close relationships. Perhaps the best help a married person can give an unmarried person is honesty about the struggles in marriage—specifically, the ways in which a spouse does *not* complete us or meet all our needs. Married or single, we can encourage one another to seek God for ultimate fulfillment and to persevere together in the pursuit of holiness.

My Spouse Will <u>*(Fill in the Blank)*</u>.

The specific expectations we can impose on our spouses have no limit. We already mentioned a specific and common one: the expectation that a spouse will listen without trying to fix the problem. Other expectations may sound like the following statements: "My spouse will share his every thought with me." "My spouse will not lie to me." "My spouse will want to watch the NFL with me every Sunday, Monday, and Thursday." "My spouse will help with the discipline of children and with the housework, laundry, and cooking." "My spouse will want to have sex often." "My spouse will not view pornography." "My spouse will plan a date night or will desire deep conversations on date nights." "My spouse will work and financially contribute to the household." "My spouse and I will go to bed together at the same time every night." "My spouse will or will not handle the budget."

As you can see from this brief list, expectations extend from daily subjects to long-term life issues. Expectations may concern relatively trivial issues, like household chores, or major moral expectations involving one's character, such as lying or pornography. It is also possible that minor matters reveal deeper issues in a marriage. When life circumstances change, expectations change as well. The expectation that a spouse will help with child care will not be realized until a child is born and the lack of assistance is experienced.

When my husband and I mentor engaged couples in our church, we always ask the couples to write down four expectations for their marriage. While all couples expect fidelity, the other three answers are often very different. We also ask them to rate their agreement with forty-three statements of expectations concerning children, household and work responsibilities, date nights, weekends, holidays, and more. The purpose of such an exercise is not only to help each couple anticipate different expectations, but to generate discussion and encourage the development of communication tools when different expectations are realized. A couple will not be able to exhaustively anticipate the different expectations each brings to the marriage. Obvious and particular important life issues, such as spiritual goals, the desire for and the number of children, where a couple will live, and so forth, should be discussed before marriage.

What about the expectation of fidelity? Does a partner in a marriage have the right to expect the other to remain faithful? Most couples enter marriage with the expectation that the spouse will be relationally and sexually faithful. The answer is yes. Fidelity is and should be the main promise expressed and witnessed at a wedding. It is the foundation of marriage. Marriage is exclusive. When we choose to marry, we are not only choosing one person; we are "forsaking all others" as explicitly stated in older marriage vows.

Yet, married couples should even hold the expectation of faithfulness cautiously and with the understanding that a sinful, well-intentioned human is making such a promise. A healthy sense of our brokenness and a continued capacity to sin motivate us to pray for a faithful heart and for the power of the Holy Spirit to empower us to preserve our promise. And we should safeguard ourselves in areas of temptation. Each spouse should flee and be wary of any thoughts or steps that shift us from that sacred promise.

One night, my husband and I were celebrating birthdays with neighbors at a local restaurant, and after dinner, most of the couples began dancing. Three unknown women began flirting and dancing around my very good friend's husband, which continued for quite some time. Later, I asked my friend if those women dancing around her husband had bothered her. She nonchalantly replied, "No, he's going home with me." Her response concerned me. Her husband's continued flirtation and dancing with those women was especially disturbing. Neither spouse seemed to sense the temptation. My husband had turned his back to those women and focused his eyes on me exclusively. He had sensed to do otherwise would be a step in the wrong direction.

In hindsight, the difference for my husband and me was only that God's Word had taught us not to be overconfident in our ability to withstand temptation, even while knowing we were wholly committed to fidelity in our marriage. No Christian begins his or her marriage with the expectation of unfaithfulness or failure. But over the years, as we watched what we thought were strong marriages between strong Christians fail, we realized that we could not be smug or arrogant about our insulation from temptation.

Two years later, my dear friend confirmed her suspicion that her dancing husband was having an affair with a co-worker. I cried with her but also remembered the seemingly unlimited confidence she had previously expressed in their relationship. The far better expectation of ourselves in marriage is not one of confidence against sin and temptation but an awareness of our vulnerability. Such awareness can help us depend on God. His Spirit can then help us stay alert to potential temptations and dangers and keep us praying and erecting safeguards to maintain our promise of faithfulness through investing in our relationship and fleeing situations of temptation. The next chapter will consider not-so-great expectations of family members beyond marriage.

Chapter 16:
Not So Great
Expectations of Family

When his family heard about this, they went to take charge of him, for they said, "He is out of his mind" (Mark 3:21).

F amilies are comprised of people related by blood, adoption, or marriage, as well as God's expression of the importance of community. Not one person is born into the world alone. By God's design, the marital family of husband and wife expands into a larger community when a child is born.

In the context of family, high or wrong expectations arise and cause damage. Romantic or idyllic ideas concerning family life persist. In our mind's eye, we see fireplaces and beautifully decorated homes with people talking, smiling, and sharing life without conflict or unmet expectations. Certainly, families can provide great joy when members feel known and loved, committed to one another through all the broken bends of life. Family can be a stable and certain shelter in a storm. Alongside the blessing of a family, however, family members can develop expectations that may harden into demands able to strain or break the relationships.

Movies depicting various degrees of dysfunctional families, some of them perhaps due to unmet expectations, have become popular.[31] The success of such movies might suggest that we appreciate the co-misery or knowledge that we are not alone in our imperfect or broken families. The Bible also speaks of pain among family members. "Do not trust a neighbor; put no confidence in a friend. Even with her who lies in your embrace be careful of your words. For a son dishonors his father, a daughter rises up against her mother, a daughter-in-law against her mother-in-law—a man's enemies are the members of his own household (Mic. 7:5–6). This passage contains strong language against ultimately trusting members of our families. Even healthy families will encounter unmet expectations.

Edith Schaeffer in *What Is a Family?*[32] describes a conflict involving her daughter Priscilla's expectation that her husband would arrive timely to a daily lunch with their family. Edith and her husband, Francis Schaeffer, were the founders of L'Abri, a retreat location in the Swiss Alps. They operated L'Abri to provide a place where persons could live for a time without distraction from the world to honestly ask spiritual questions and seek after God. Every day, Edith and Francis spent hours teaching, discussing, and working alongside people from all over the world. Their daughter Priscilla and son-in-law John participated in this work as well. Since they were so busy, Priscilla hoped her husband and their three children could carve family time in a forty-five-minute lunch period. Priscilla reasoned that since they lived, worked, and conversed with so many people, it was of great importance to have this daily lunchtime with only their children and each other. Her husband, however, was often late to lunch, leaving the family with only minutes remaining before the children had to return to school and Priscilla and her husband to work. Since Priscilla and John had different expectations as to the importance of family time at lunch, many expressions of anger, disappointment, and conflict filled the remaining fifteen minutes. The harmonious family lunch hour was destroyed. Priscilla finally realized she had to surrender her expectation that her husband would arrive on time. As a birthday present to her husband, she promised that for two months, she would not scold him or be mad when he arrived late for lunch. Whatever family time did occur at lunch became positive and full of joy instead of anger and disappointment.

This honest story reveals how unchecked expectations can damage relationships. This story also reveals the truth that each person in a relationship must choose to maintain the relationship and to what extent they must do so. While families create permanent biological connections with each other, the relational connection in a family may not endure even among its members. Some of a family's disruptions may be caused by wrong expectations.

My Family Will Always Be There for Me

One high expectation involves the idea that family members will be "there" for us in times of trouble, adversity, or celebration. Yet, family members sometimes fail to show up or give the desired help when we are in need. Proverbs 17:17 says, "A friend loves at all times and a brother is born for times of adversity." This proverb seems to suggest that friends will love you, but your family will substantially come through in times of adversity. When different expectations collide, conflict and hurt result, grudges are held, bitterness takes root, and eventually, relationships may die, even those among family.

King David expressed his disappointed expectation when his family, the tribe of Judah, did not act in a certain way at a time of celebration. He had expected his family to be the first to welcome him back as king after he had defeated Absalom. He expected the people of Judah to restore him to the throne, not the other ten tribes of Israel, who had initiated escorting David back. In 2

Samuel 19:11-12, David sent a message to the priests to ask the elders of Judah, "Why should you be the last to bring the king back to his palace, since what is being said throughout Israel has reached the king at his quarters? You are my brothers, my own flesh and blood. So why should you be the last to bring back the king?" David thought his family should have been there to return him to the throne in Jerusalem. David's expectation was seemingly created because of his family ties to Judah. The tribe of Judah agreed and subsequently decided to escort the king back to the palace, which then offended the tribes of Israel. The ten tribes later divided from Judah. Although we do not know the precise and entire cause of this division, perhaps this offense that David's expectation had created, played a small role in Israel's separation from Judah.

My Family Will Act in a Certain Way

The previous expectation expressed the vague idea that family would be "there" or be present to help in trouble or rejoice in celebration. In other situations, we develop specific ideas about how families should act. Many examples could be offered. When a parent dies, the surviving children often have different expectations as to property distribution or funeral plans. Due to conflicting ideas about a family's estate distribution, many siblings no longer relate after the death of their parents. In the story discussed in the introduction, Elizabeth's failure to meet Ellen's expectations for abundant communication about their father's estate caused damage to their relationship. As a result, Ellen disengaged from the relationship with her sister and began to suspect Elizabeth was stealing from the estate. In another instance, a mother and daughter may find they have widely varying expectations about the daughter's wedding. These examples display the potential damage when we hold ironclad expectations of other family members. When we view our perspective as more important, wrong expectations may cause the loss of relationships.

Another common area with incompatible family expectations involves holiday celebrations. What often begins as fun traditions can soon become demands or expectations. Family traditions are generally very good; they provide certainty and stable foundations which strengthen our identity and security in belonging. But as families grow and change, holiday gatherings by necessity must also grow and change.

Every other year on Thanksgiving, my extended family tries to continue the tradition of eating dinner together by sharing the same table. No buffet is allowed; we must sit down and share the same table. My earliest memory of this tradition began when there were eleven of us around the table. Last Thanksgiving, to hold on to this tradition, we sat fifty-nine people around multiple lined-up, end-to-end tables. Only my sister's house is large enough to accommodate such a huge table, which of course means she must continue to host instead of sharing the responsibility as we had done in the past. Consequently, my sister unfairly suffers the stress of accommodating this many people. We have fought long and hard to keep the tradition of sitting down at the same table at Thanksgiving dinner. My niece's sentiment expresses the value: "Being with everyone is the most important thing. We have to find a way to work it out." I love that my niece values our Thanksgiving tradition. But as families grow and change, traditions sometimes must also adapt. Through marriage, new families are created, and each spouse brings additional extended family into the mix, along with different holiday expectations. I am sure we will not find a way to forever seat all of us at the same table for Thanksgiving. We can work to maintain traditions, but we must not let different expectations destroy relationships with our extended family.

When we feel hurt, angry, or disappointed with family, it is helpful to examine our feelings. Sometimes the strength or certainty of our feelings causes us to confuse an unmet expectation with an actual wrong. To avoid this confusion, we should evaluate our thoughts in light of God's Word. Perhaps ask yourself, "Have I been morally wronged, or have my expectations been damaged?"

Does God's Word say we must gather on holidays? He instituted feasts and commanded gatherings for the Israelites. Those festivals served God's purposes for Israel and simultaneously encouraged good relationships and a strong identity as God's people. The feasts in the Old Testament suggest pausing our routines to gather and remember God's goodness together is a wonderful practice. Yet, God did not mandate specific traditions for families. Our upbringing likely taught us that family must always gather on holidays. Can we find new ways to uphold God's important values of family and relationships while discovering new traditions or ways to celebrate? We can embrace a necessary change in tradition, knowing that in eternity, we will have tables and mansions and time long enough to fit all who belong to the family of Christ to celebrate together God's immeasurable goodness through His Son.

Chapter 17:
Parent/Child Expectations

May the Lord cause you to flourish, both you and your children (Ps. 115:14).

Although a family relationship, the parent-child relationship is treated separately from other familial relations due to the unique expectations that arise within it. In this relationship, both parties may grow wrong expectations. Parents often begin their roles with newborn infants and set unrealistically high expectations of themselves as the perfect parent. As parents, we determine to fill our child's world with wonderful experiences, teach them about God, cook healthy meals, maintain a clean house, always exercise appropriate discipline, and make sure our child feels loved! Parents may not only begin with high expectations of themselves, but they may also grow high expectations of their children. In the parental control tower, we may demand near perfection through unrealistically high expectations. One overarching and common but often unspoken expectation of parents may sound like this: "If I parent correctly, my children will turn out well." "Well" is defined according to a parent's particular plan for each child but usually includes happiness; education; good health; and success in sports, music, art, academics, or all of the above. The Christian version of success adds a spiritual dimension.

If I Parent Them Correctly, My Children Will Become Followers of Jesus

In print, this expectation seems too high. A Christian knows salvation is a free gift that God offers to each individual, which they can either receive or reject. No one can cause another to choose to enter a personal relationship with God. Certainly, Christian parenting involves teaching a child about Jesus and living out the reality of such a relationship. Such involvement can go a long way toward helping a child see his personal need for Jesus.

Parents are commanded to teach their children. "Train a child in the way he should go, and when he is old he will not turn from it" (Prov. 22:6). This proverb gives the impression and many have understood this verse to say that if the parent properly trains the child, he or she will eventually arrive and stay "in the way he should go." However, proverbs are not guarantees. Bible commentators warn not to assume that proverbs are unconditional promises but to understand that they only tell what may generally happen. One commentator expressed the point of Proverb 22:6. "This verse should not be considered a promise but a general principle of education and commitment."[33] Knowing this passage shored up my commitment to teach and train my children. It encouraged me to persevere in what I hoped was Christ-centered parenting. Yet, many committed Christians have children who have not chosen to follow Christ while other children come to know the Lord despite an anti-Christian upbringing.

What should a Christian parent do? Of course, there are helpful books that offer advice. I remember feeling excited when I found a book entitled *How to Lead Your Child to Christ*.[34] I devoured it, thinking if I could just do all the things this book said to do, then my children would come to Christ. Since I no longer have this book, I attempted to find it through the internet. Immediately, another title popped up: *How to Bring Your Children to Christ & Keep Them There: Avoiding the Tragedy of False Conversion.*[35] This title grabbed my attention because it expressed the hope of every Christian parent. A parent who understands the supremacy of Christ and the life-and-death importance of their child's decision to receive God's gift of Jesus desires nothing more for their child than to receive salvation and to enjoy the wonderful blessings of living in relationship with God. But the verbs *bring* and *keep* are beyond the control of the parent. It is not fair to criticize the title of a book I have not read. If my children were small, I would likely read this book to glean help in the difficult task of parenting, especially to help point them to Christ. However, the title promises too much. Many parenting books provide beneficial insights, and I would recommend all sorts of reading. Yet, no parenting book or plan will in itself make our kids turn out "all right" or keep them following Christ. Frankly, I have enough to manage to keep my own heart from wandering from Christ. Parents have no ultimate control over the long- or short-term custody of a child's heart. The idea that they have control builds an unwarranted expectation.

When children are young, parents have some measure of control that we hope quickly gives way to influence when they are older. Regarding the choice to begin a relationship with Christ, we can pray, talk, teach, and model the reality of a love relationship with Christ. We should employ every possible means to show our child the wondrous God we know. As parents, we are responsible to God, who commands us to teach, discipline, and train our children, but not exasperate them. We look to cooperate with and trust God, who is pursuing a relationship with our children. We must guard our thoughts to discern when any of our good desires have turned into not-so-great expectations. Such expectations overly burden the parenting task and compel unhealthy control of the child, which could potentially push the child further away from God.

Not only can we develop expectations of ourselves as parents, but we can also cultivate expectations of our children. We expect young children to obey, and we want them to behave as we have taught them; when they do not, we impose upon them appropriate consequences. We expect politeness and gratitude; we expect clean rooms and good grades. We try to train them in godly character. All of these are good parenting desires, but parents must guard themselves against the high expectation that their children will always do what they have been taught. Our children inherited the same sinful nature that afflicts all humans. We might be surprised in the ways they sin, which may make us sad and concerned for them, but we should not overreact and expect sinless perfection from them. Any expectation for perfect obedience must be surrendered. It is vital that we pray and hope that our children are persuaded that God's design for life is best.

When children become adults, our expectations of them change. We no longer expect even imperfect obedience, but we naturally hope for a continuing relationship with adult children. Such a desire can ripen into a demand.

My Adult Children Will Want a Relationship with Me

In the beginning of a parent-child relationship, the parent will sustain the connection with the child. Over time, the joy of being loved and desired by their child can develop into a demand or expectation for the child to return their love. Or, a parent may expect appreciation and gratitude, or a level of investment in the relationship that is different than what the adult child desires. When a child first attends college, she may think, *If my mom wants to spend time with me, preferably at a mall with her wallet in tow, she can call and let me know, and if I have time and need some stuff, maybe I will show up.* The parent may think: *I have done so much for my child, including payment of her college tuition. I am interested in her daily life; she should call and share everything going on in her life.* One can readily see the conflict in these different expectations. Most often, adult children and parents navigate a new sort of relationship that works, but when the transition involves greater pain and hurt than normal, the cause might be different or unmet expectations. During parenting, we gradually lose most-favored status in our child's life to friends in middle school and high school. We know purposeful parenting aims to help children grow independent from us and dependent on God, but from the first time our children prefer someone else, pain can seep into our hearts.

This expectation for more time with adult children is common. I remember the joy my mom expressed when all her adult children were home, even though it puzzled me at the time. At one point, I was feeling particularly distant from my grown children and sad about the relational distance after so many years of close daily interactions. I prayed, silently complaining to God that my children had forgotten my service to them. God's response to me was quick. He reminded me that he had forgiven the people who put him on the Cross. He reminded me that he had loved, served, and washed the feet of men who, during his deepest hour of need, had abandoned him. He reminded me that while *I* was a sinner, he died for me (Rom. 5:8). Even though God rescued me, how many times do I continue to ignore or fail to appreciate him?

Through my high expectations of my children, I understood a little, a micro millionth, of the suffering Christ endured for me, his rebellious child. Once again, I was reminded that only God does not disappoint. All of God's children are called to the same mission as Christ: to love people, including our children, without regard to how they love in return, and then to offer this love to God as a way to reflect his amazing, life-giving, and unfailing love. The alternative spells certain death to these relationships.

Children's Expectations of Parents

Conversely, children can form wrong, unhealthy, or high expectations of their parents. For example, a child who receives many gifts may begin to expect and even demand gifts. My parents were not poor, but there was no extra money from a mailman's paycheck and a stay-at-home mom of six children. When I accompanied my mom to the store, many times I would ask her for something, and her answer was always no. I learned not to expect anything extra at the store, so I stopped asking. My parent's choice or inability to give gifts beyond meeting my needs created a low expectation for extras. This low expectation helped to increase my gratitude when I received birthday or Christmas gifts. In hindsight, the best gift my parents gave me was this low expectation to receive. Of course, I have struggled with materialism, but my parents' actions in this area helped.

With the wealth we possess and the consequent ability to give to our children, as parents, we perhaps unwittingly promote an expectation or entitlement for many possessions. Adult children might expect financial help if parents frequently give them money. They may begin to depend on the help and demand their parents to bail them out of trouble, financial or otherwise. A parent's desire to continue to be needed by adult children may fuel unhealthy support. Of course, it is not wrong to help adult children at times. But it is important to recognize that repeated actions often create expectations, so parents should give thoughtful consideration to the long-term best course of action before a decision to help is made.

Each parent-child relationship is unique, so within these relationships, many potential expectations should be addressed. Not-so-great expectations in the lifelong parent-child relationship will continue to require consideration, gracious communication, and forgiveness.

Like family relationships, our life at work consumes a great portion of time and relational investment. It is likely that relationships at work also contain wrong expectations.

Chapter 18:
Not So Great Expectations in Employment

The ground is cursed because of you. You will eat from it by means of painful labor all the days of your life (Gen. 3:17).

Expectations are valid when a relationship delineates them implicitly or explicitly. Whether through written contracts, promises, verbal instructions or repeated behavior, the parties may agree on expectations. The employment relationship provides an example when the employer promises to pay the employee and provide benefits in exchange for work. The employee may legitimately expect to be paid and endure consequences for failure to work. Other expectations in employment are not as obvious or appropriate. We might expect a job to be lastingly fulfilling and stimulating, yet the Bible communicates that as a result of the fall of mankind, work will be difficult at times (Gen. 3:17-19). Some of our dissatisfaction at work may result from unfairness, but a very common but not-so-great expectation concerns the desire to be valued for our contribution. The complaint may be simply stated as follows.

My Employer Doesn't Appreciate Me

Many workers anticipate difficulties in their employment but remain unaware of the common expectation to be appreciated for good work. Some employers may regularly notice hard work and excellent performance, some during a yearly review, and others not at all. An employee may labor hard and long without encouragement, whereas typically, a mistake or poor performance will garner an employer's immediate attention. A student in a class on expectations wrote of her struggle in this area.

> *My wrong or unmet expectation is work-related. I am constantly thinking my way is the best way. I expect my boss to see my hard work and reward me. Nowhere in my contract did it say that if I managed these other teams or if I put in extra effort, I was guaranteed a raise. The damage this mind-set caused was bitterness and resentment toward my "lazy" coworkers and anger and disrespect toward my boss. The truth is I don't deserve anything, and my reward for working is the paycheck I bring home. On Friday, I placed my hope in God, and in my monthly one-on-one with my boss, I told him how I was feeling and apologized for having such high expectations. He said he did appreciate all my hard work, and then he told me what I didn't know was that he had put in for a raise for me last week because he thought I deserved it. I cried a little because I felt like God was coming through for me.*

Like this young student described, the expectation that work will be appreciated can cause many problems. She humbly admitted bitterness and resentment against her co-workers and boss. Some have sought employment elsewhere only to be disappointed again when the new employer failed to notice.

Is the expectation for appreciation or gratitude for good work legitimate? Should we expect praise? Jesus addressed a similar question in Luke 17:9-10. After describing a common work situation in the first century of a servant plowing or looking after sheep, Jesus asked, "Would he thank the servant because he did what he was told to do? So you also, when you have done everything you were told to do should say, 'We are unworthy servants; we have only done our duty.'" The words of Jesus suggest we should not expect appreciation from employers. We may or may not receive notice and praise.

Once again, the biblical answer is to entrust ourselves to God, to live, love, and work with a vertical perspective. "Whatever you do, work at it with all your heart, as working for the Lord, not for human masters, since you know that you will receive an inheritance from the Lord as a reward. It is the Lord Christ you are serving" (Col. 3:23-24). If we offer our work to God, praise and appreciation from employers will be less necessary. God will notice and provide the reward of praise when truly needed and in a manner that lets us know that he has seen our work. The student was overjoyed when she experienced God "coming through" for her. God explicitly promises the reward of inheritance. If the praise does not come in this life, it will surely come in our eternal life, for God always keeps his promise. "Well done good and faithful servant" (Matt. 25:21, 23) will be worth much more from God, our eternal Father, than any earthly employer.

Chapter 19:
Not So Great Expectations of Institutions

Do not put your trust in princes, in human beings who cannot save (Ps. 146:3).

When individuals fail to live up to expectations, many invest their hope in organizations or institutions. Organizations, which are constituted by people for a common purpose, affect all of our lives in the form of government, private corporations, or the church.

What expectations do we have of the government? We may expect the government to protect us from enemy invaders, provide services for citizens, build infrastructure, punish crime, and administer justice through a legal system. We indirectly pay for these services through taxation. Some individuals may expect the government to meet additional needs, including many social assistance plans that are aptly named "entitlement programs." Fundamental disagreements concern the areas and extent to which the government should provide for its residents. Some citizens are disappointed by their government's failure to meet their expectations.

Similar to their reliance on the government, several people place hope in widely divergent political organizations or parties. They invest time, emotional and financial resources, and votes in a certain candidate or political organization, expecting ultimate solutions.

A corporation, if organized for profit by its charter, will act according to this profit purpose. Any expectation outside of its stated corporate goal is unrealistic.

When people work together and pool their resources, much can be accomplished, and our lives are unavoidably entwined with many institutions. Yet, humans direct all corporations, governments, or organizations, political or otherwise, with all the frailty and flaws which have been repeatedly discussed. The Bible channels our hope away from any human endeavor and onto God alone. "No king is saved by the size of his army; no warrior escapes by his great strength. A horse is a vain hope for deliverance despite all its great strength it cannot save. But the eyes of the LORD are on those who fear him, on those whose hope is in his unfailing love" (Ps. 33:16-18). We would do well to remember that an army, a strong horse, or any manifestation of these things in the form of a human institution, is ultimately a vain hope.

The Church as an Organization

The Church Will Always Represent God Well

As an organization of Jesus Christ, the church has a different aim than that of a secular institution. The purpose of the church is multifaceted, but it may be summarized as to "proclaim the excellencies of Him who has called you out of darkness into His marvelous light" (1 Pet. 2:9, NASB). Yet, even on its best days, the church, a group of consecrated-to-God humans, will not accurately proclaim Christ's excellencies. I have heard it said, "I would be a Christian

117

except for the Christian church." The verdict of history would be mixed: the crusades, inquisition, and scandals versus the abolition of slavery, creation of hospitals, and more. Like any secular organization, the church is comprised of sinners, but in the church, God has redeemed sinners for a love relationship with himself. Thus, a realistic expectation of the church as an institution includes, just as with individuals, both sinful behavior and otherworldly love. When particular situations discredit the church, we should not be surprised—we may be saddened but not surprised. Conversely, much quiet beauty and dignity are displayed through the church of Christ, which is often ignored or unseen rather than balanced against its problems.

The Church Exists to Meet My Needs

Individual members of the church institution may possess wrong expectations that arise as a result of a fundamental misunderstanding of the church's purpose. If the church exists to primarily meet our spiritual needs, to entertain or provide problem-free social contacts, then all sorts of incorrect expectations will arise and result in various disappointments: the teachings are not good enough; the music is not great; these people are not interesting or nice enough. Upon first *joining* a church, quality biblically based teachings and a sense that a church "fits" may be legitimate considerations. But once planted in a church, it is hard to think of a reason why one should voluntarily leave, apart from the church teaching false doctrine. This is true because God has planted us in our church. 1 Corinthians 12:18 states, "But in fact God has placed the parts in the body, every one of them, just as he wanted them to be." Because God has placed us in a certain church, we should not lightly consider a change. If we find ourselves "church hopping" and cannot express a specific legitimate reason to leave our current church, an unrealistic expectation may be the cause of our dissatisfaction. If complaints such as "this church does not meet my needs" or "I do not like the way they are doing things now" recur, these thoughts may signal a not-so-great expectation. God, of course, may sometimes *call* people to leave and attend a different church. However, leaving the church where God has established us should be considered the exception, not the norm. It is far too easy to leave a church when difficulty and conflict arise. God likely wants to work through those challenges with us. He may want us to resolve conflict or initiate innovation and change in our current church, or he might just want us to persevere and trust him in the place he has put us.

Furthermore, the church primarily exists not only to proclaim Christ but to serve and bless others. Plain and simple, the church is not about me and my individual desires. It is about God and us corporately. The church provides a wonderful community, a spiritual family, which helps us belong, heal, and grow in Christlikeness. Often, through the church, God will meet our needs and provide us with many blessings that abound as a byproduct of belonging to a local church. But the expectation of each member should eventually be to primarily give, sacrifice, and bless others rather than to receive blessings. To expect fundamental satisfaction from any organization, including the church, will result in much disappointment.

This chapter concludes the consideration of various expectations of people in many manifestations. While only the most prevalent expectations were addressed, the possibilities in the ways we impose not-so-great expectations on individuals and organizations are endless. The hope is this survey of common expectations better equips us to recognize them in our relationships.

Summary of Biblical Relational Principles

Since we have covered much ground concerning the not-so-great expectations of people, let us end this section by summarizing and restating biblical principles that give us hope. When relationships with people are based on God's perspective rather than our expectations, they can thrive! If half of us allow God to empower us, and if we live according to even half of these principles half of the time, our relationships will succeed and testify to the reality of an amazing God!

1. First, turn to God with your emotions. Express your hurt, anger, and disappointment to him. Thank him for his grace, forgiveness, unfailing love, and commitment to your growth in character and healthy relationships. Consciously and decidedly entrust yourself to him.

2. Look at the log in your eye, specifically searching for wrong, high, or unrealistic expectations. Consider how you want to be treated. Give the benefit of the doubt, forgive, forbear, and pray for the power to treat the perceived offender accordingly.

3. Try to obey the "one another" commands in God's Word. Remember these standards are *for us* to apply *to ourselves*, not to impose on others. They tell us how God would have us respond when expectations are not met.

4. Guard yourself against emotional self-protection. Fill your mind with the truth of God's all-encompassing love for you. His love calls us to initiate and move toward others for their good. Like Jesus, entrust yourself, your safety, and your well-being to God but be willing to die to self for others.

5. In ongoing relationships, and after seeking God's direction, carefully communicate desires and expectations with humility.

6. With your brothers and sisters in Christ, work hard to preserve unity, knowing God's glory to the watching world may be at stake. Realize that sometimes it is better to be wronged or cheated than to dispute with your spiritual siblings (1 Cor. 6:6).

7. Remember Proverbs 19:11, which suggests our own reflected glory may be at stake: "A person's wisdom yields patience; it is to one's glory to overlook an offense."

Chapter 20: Not So Great Expectations of Life

What we anticipate seldom occurs; what we least expected generally happens. — *Benjamin Disraeli, Henrietta Temple*

If interviewed, most people could point to many unexpected events that have occurred in life, both wonderful and heartbreaking. Life truly is an adventure in the sense that we do not know what lies over the next hill. At the time of publication, we are in the midst of a global pandemic, not something most of us expected in times of modernity and medical advancement. The pandemic has left many shaken, despondent, and discouraged. The confident ground on which we once stood has moved beneath us.

Although discouragement is part of ordinary life, sometimes unnecessary or extreme disappointment results from unrecognized and unfulfilled expectations. For example, early in life, we may have been taught that anything is attainable if we work hard. God commands us to work, not to build bigger barns, but to take care of the needs of our household, win the respect of outsiders, and have something to share with others. Idleness is chastised and is the opposite of Paul's example to the Thessalonians (2 Thess. 3:6-10), and hard work is a value expressed in the Bible (Prov. 14:23). Yet, the overemphasis of hard work has left many disappointed. The hard work of a five-foot man will not likely result in an NBA contract. Nor will hard work always equal career or monetary success. In the book *Outliers,* author Malcolm Gladwell argues well that fortunate circumstances often beyond our control contribute much to success.

Another common expectation is that life will yield happiness and contentment if we secure the best job or marry the right person. Trying to improve our lives is not wrong. However, a continual seeking of perfect circumstances might reveal we expect this earthly life to produce heavenly contentment.

We sometimes unknowingly believe that if we arrange our lives just right, we will be lastingly satisfied. Jesus told a parable of a wealthy man with high expectations of life. This farmer enlarged his barns so he could store more grain and goods, thinking such wealth would make him happy. He said to himself, "You have plenty of good things laid up for many years. Take life easy; eat, drink and be merry" (Luke 12:19).

A continual seeking of perfect circumstances might reveal we expect this earthly life to produce heavenly contentment.

Sadly, we may live life echoing this farmer's sentiment. We may say, "If only I could graduate, obtain a high-paying job, get married, have children, help the children to sleep through the night or get on a schedule, find a part-time job, enjoy my work, save more, or retire..." Repeatedly, discontentment may surface through various seasons of life. We are determined to search for the best and perfect life. When these good desires inordinately drive our time, thoughts, and energy, such drive may evidence a wrong expectation for complete fulfillment and satisfaction in this life. God promises we will only find abundant life in him and perfect contentment in the next life. The wealthy farmer's plan to build a perfect life ended with God's assessment. "You fool! This very night your life will be demanded from you" (12:20).

American Expectations

Life expectations in Western culture, particularly in America, assume a heightened character, since our founding documents have taught us that life, liberty, and the pursuit of happiness is our right. To pursue these may be our right as Americans, but should we expect that we will obtain them or keep them? An entire package of expectations falls under the umbrella of the American dream: to own your own home, graduate from college, thus ensuring a well-paying and fulfilling job, and more. In short, we want to be comfortable, healthy, and reasonably wealthy. In America, most of us unconsciously live with the idea that we should have these things. We may have to work for them, but eventually, we should have them, as well as the life we design.

We may also unwittingly expect life to be free of hassles. This expectation of a problem-free life may manifest itself through extreme frustration with computer or internet failures, car issues, or the breakdown of any mechanical appliance. Most of the time, these systems work well, but our reactions during mishaps might expose that we expect them to work *all* the time. More than perfectly working equipment, however, we can sometimes find we expect a certain lifestyle or measure of success.

A Successful Lifestyle

The not-so-great expectation of success, however defined, differs from God's perspective of success. In our culture, the answer for success is peace, affluence, comfort, entertainment, and travel. We want autonomy and wonderful experiences. America's long period of affluence has enabled us to more quickly and easily build these expectations of success compared to other parts of the world. The good life has caused us to expect the good life, and we often assume the good life should continue. Job, who experienced long prosperity prior to adversity, was not different in his expectation. "I thought, 'I will die in my own house, my days as numerous as the grains of sand. My roots will reach to the water, and the dew will lie all night on my branches. My glory will not fade; the bow will be ever new in my hand'" (29:18–20).

When we expect life to always give us the goods, we ask more of life than it can deliver. When doing this, we worship life instead of the Giver of life. Discontent, we miss the joy of the present goodness and the opportunity to trust God in our current situation. We pour our energy into a "broken cistern that cannot hold water" (Jer. 2:13). In short, we waste the life that God has given us. What then is the biblical standard of success?

When my very dear friend was approaching her late thirties, she realized her life's desire to bear children was not likely to happen. She expressed, "Life is short. If I can serve God better by remaining single and without children, then that is best and what I want more than anything." My friend admitted she battled to keep this perspective even though this perspective reflects biblical truth. "'Truly I tell you,' Jesus replied, 'no one who has left home or brothers or sisters or mother or father or children or fields for me and the gospel will fail to receive a hundred times as much in this present age: homes, brothers, sisters, mothers, children, and fields—along with persecutions—and in the age to come eternal life'" (Mark 10:29–30). Success in God's view is faithfulness to him above all else. Whenever we put God as our first priority, he will multiply whatever we have lost or given up. A hundred times' return is a successful investment. God promises us more than abundant life now. As Christians, we already possess every spiritual blessing (Eph. 1:3), yet we easily confuse spiritual blessings with perfect-life expectations.

God's chosen people, the Israelites, were assured a good life on earth if they obeyed and followed God (Deut. 4:40; 5:33; 6:3, 18; 12:28; Isa. 3:10; Jer. 7:23). However, because they did not obey and follow him, they experienced many unnecessary hardships. Perhaps the way God was setting apart his nation and his dealings with the Israelites is also a source of our "good life" expectations.

Under the new covenant that Christ inaugurated, God did not promise Christians a rose garden or a Garden of Eden. He did not promise that life would always "go well" for His followers. Although we currently enjoy many extraordinary blessings, including the Spirit of God as our Helper, God's Word indicates our life expectations should include suffering and persecution, at least insofar as we practice and proclaim our faith. D. A. Carson states:

> *The fact that many in the West have for so long been largely exempt from the worst features of such persecution has let us lower our guard—even Christians may think that a hassle-free life is something that society owes us. But as the Judeo-Christian heritage of the West weakens, we may one day be caught up in realities that missions specialists know but that the rest of us sometimes ignore: the last century and a half have seen more converts, and more martyrs, than the first eighteen centuries combined.* [36]

The Bible clearly warns, "In fact, everyone who wants to live a godly life in Christ Jesus will be persecuted" (2 Tim. 3:12). In some way and to some extent, suffering and persecution should be the legitimate expectation of every Christian because this fallen life cannot wholly deliver perfect happiness, and also simply because we follow Christ. However, this life does not have the last word. Jesus tells us to rest in him. "I have told you these things, so that in me you may have peace. In this world, you will have trouble. But take heart! I have overcome the world" (John 16:33).

Life Will Be Fair

If there is one mantra I often repeated in my child-rearing years, it was "don't expect life to be fair!" This was almost always uttered in response to one or more of my children's complaints of "that's not fair!" Sometimes my response was a knee-jerk reaction due to impatience, but I did want to consciously build a low expectation of fairness within my children. Even when we are young, our hearts instinctively long for justice. When little children are harmed, when the elderly are mistreated, or when we experience a personal affront, we feel outraged. Evidence of unfairness is plentiful. The hard-working, God-fearing, moral person seems to endure endless tragedy, while the wicked, greedy, or otherwise evil person seems to flourish without any apparent trouble.

Psalm 73 expresses this struggle. "For I envied the arrogant when I saw the prosperity of the wicked. They have no struggles; their bodies are healthy and strong. They are free from the burdens common to man; they are not plagued by human ills" (vv. 3–6). Through many verses, the Psalmist continues to wrestle with apparent unfairness.

The realization that we live in a broken world should prevent us from having an expectation of fairness. Perfect justice cannot be attained in this life. We can use court systems, laws, and enforcement officers when appropriate to attempt justice now. We can even serve in social organizations that endeavor to bless and elevate the unfairly oppressed and downtrodden. While all these institutions are useful and can be wonderful, godly instruments to bring a measure of fairness to bear in this life, ultimate justice will only be attained when Christ returns and God reigns at the end of autonomous human history.

However, *God* is completely just and fair. As his followers and representatives, we are also to be fair and just. "And what does the Lord require of you? To act justly and to love mercy and to walk humbly with your God" (Mic. 6:8). To obey God and represent him well, we treat others fairly.

When we demand justice for ourselves, we need to remember that God has given us mercy for our offenses. Although God's justice demands death for sin (Rom. 6:23), Christ satisfied this justice. Remembering we have received mercy will bend us to show mercy to others when we are wronged.

Nathan, a prophet at the time of King David, related a story to David that illustrates our need for mercy more than justice. Nathan tells of a rich man who stole from a poor man his one and only ewe lamb. Upon hearing this, David angrily cried out for justice (2 Sam. 12:5-6). Nathan revealed that David was the thief in his affair with Bathsheba, the wife of Uriah, who David later had murdered to conceal his sin. At that moment, David recognized his sin against God and his utter need for mercy. Similarly, we recognize that it was not fair for Christ to bear our sins, but it was merciful.

God's sovereignty and generosity answer, at least in part, perceived unfairness. In the parable of the vineyard, when the workers complained because they were paid the same amount despite the different length of hours worked, the owner's response indicated God is generous. "Or are you envious because I am generous?" (Matt. 20:15). As God's ambassadors, we should strive to be fair and just to others, but we should not expect fairness for ourselves, nor do we want God to be just toward us. We want God to be gracious and generous. And he is.

Health

A common area in which we develop lofty life expectations is our physical and mental health. We expect to always feel physically well and happy. When we do not, we think we are entitled to immediate help, such as medicine or surgery. Medical assistance and ordinary attempts to alleviate pain or sadness are not wrong, but when we have an underlying expectation that continual and constant physical and mental health rests in this life, we need to examine the legitimacy of this belief.

Another not-so-great expectation concerns healthy habits. Exercise, good nutrition, and refraining from smoking will ensure a good quality of life and forestall or eliminate death. Of course, these practices contribute to good health, and the Bible teaches us to steward all God has given us, including our bodies. But the marketing of drugs and the proliferation of medical information to consumers perhaps leads to the belief that every illness demands a fix or that we can ultimately and completely control our health.

Disease, decay, aging, and death are all unalterably parts of this life, which renders the absence of physical or mental pain an unrealistic expectation. For the next life, we have hope and a promise for the absence of pain. "There will be no more death or mourning or crying or pain, for the old order of things has passed away" (Rev. 21:4). Only when we are God's co-tenants on the re-created earth can we expect the perfect working of our new bodies and minds.

In the meantime, we hope in God. We can appropriate medical care as a useful resource and perhaps as the means through which God will work. However, we should always pray to our Father and Master Designer of our bodies for all our needs, including our physical and mental health. Remember the difference between King Hezekiah and King Asa. Hezekiah asked God for healing, while Asa did not. In the end, Hezekiah was given fifteen additional years of life. As God's beloved creatures and children, we should do no less than Hezekiah.

I Should Be Successful in Ministry

As Christians, we may develop life expectations that are unique to the faith, such as, that we will have success in ministry or that we will serve in a particular ministry role. We consider evangelism a success when others begin a personal relationship with Jesus Christ. We consider the church a success when churches grow and discipleship produces more Christ-like individuals who are convinced of the worth of wholeheartedly following God. God desires these things. While these are wonderful desires, they are wrong expectations. We have no control over another's freedom to choose a relationship or to walk with God. The growth of God's church is explicitly within his sovereignty (1 Cor. 3:6). We work to advance God's purposes in the world, but we may not often achieve success from a human viewpoint. If growth and salvation are the only measures of success, ministry becomes overwhelmingly discouraging. Under a man-centered view, Isaiah, Jeremiah, and Ezekiel were not successful in turning Israel and Judah back to God.

In the New Testament, we are repeatedly told that some responded to Jesus and the gospel message of the apostles, and some did not. Even after the people witnessed the raising of a dead man, Lazarus, the Bible reports mixed results. "Therefore many of the Jews who had come to visit Mary, and had seen what Jesus did, put their faith in him. But some of them went to the Pharisees and told them what Jesus had done" (John 11:45-46). The same is true of Paul. "Some were convinced by what he said, but others would not believe" (Acts 28:24). For more examples of a mixed response to Paul's message, see Acts 14:1-2; 17:4-5, 12; and 34. If Jesus and Paul could not convince everyone to believe, it is unreasonable to think we will always be successful in this task.

In *any* ministry we undertake with him and for him, God promises success defined as bearing fruit if we rest in him (John 15:5). Our work in the Lord is never in vain (1 Cor. 15:58). His Word promises we will reap a harvest. "Let us not become weary in doing good for at the proper time we will reap a harvest if we do not give up" (Gal. 6:9). We might not presently see or recognize the fruit or the harvest, for it may not be the proper time, but we can trust God's Word. From God's perspective, success in ministry is about perseverance in faithfulness and rest in him.

I Should Have This Role in Ministry

As followers of Christ, we might also define success as possessing a particular role in ministry. This attitude might manifest when we feel envy at another's role or we belittle our own position. The truth is that God graciously invites us to co-labor with him; we have no right to demand a different or specific function. We are actors on God's stage, gifted to play a part in his story. When we envy the gifting of others or their role in ministry, God's Word gently reminds us that he has given all of us the privileged appointment as ambassadors, regardless of our function (2 Cor. 5:20).

In Scripture, God not so gently denounced the demand of a different ministry position. In Numbers chapter 16, three Levites who were already performing important duties at the tabernacle, the dwelling place of God, complained that they wanted to be priests as well. Moses scolded them, saying:

> *Isn't it enough for you that the God of Israel has separated you from the rest of the Israelite community and brought you near himself to do the work at the Lord's tabernacle*

and to stand before the community and minister to them?
He has brought you and all your fellow Levites near him-
self, but now you are trying to get the priesthood too. It is
against the LORD *that you and all your followers have*
banded together. (Num. 16:9–11)

When we complain or dismiss our gifted role in ministry, we
are ultimately railing against God, not our church leaders. God, in
his sovereignty and wisdom, decides each of our roles. Whatever
role God grants to us, we can trust his promise that our lives will
bear fruit and reap a harvest if we persevere; our lives will matter.
Whenever our role seems insignificant or ineffective, we need to
recall these promises.

In all areas of life and ministry, we cannot expect perfection
or particular roles or results. Yet, over time, our lives will become
stories of supernatural fruit-bearing as we persevere in faith and
hope. In the meantime, we look forward to the best life after we
die. We remember the promised perfect paradise of God's presence
for his children.

Another perspective describes our lives as comedies. In literature,
the difference between a tragedy and a comedy depends not on what
happens throughout the play but on how the story ends. We know
the end. Our life stories are comedies. Let us laugh and rejoice!

Chapter 21:
Rehabilitate Not So Great
Expectations

We take captive every thought to make it obedient to
Christ (2 Cor. 10:5).

At this point, we have explored many common expectations.
We have recognized the damage that expectations cause to
relationships, joy, and effectiveness in God's work. The question
is overdue. Is there a remedy for not-so-great expectations? Is the
answer to simply have no expectations at all? Alexander Pope suggested a ninth beatitude. "Blessed is the man who expects nothing,
for he shall never be disappointed."[37] I do not believe we can live
without expectations. Wrong ideas continually sprout and grow like
weeds in a garden, and they mutate according to situations and seasons of life. Yet, we can cultivate realistic expectations and rehabilitate the not-so-great ones.

Rehabilitation restores one to health through training and
therapy. Therapy is often painful and always a process. The word
rehabilitation captures both the ongoing struggle to revise expectations as they are exposed, and it includes hope for restoration to
greater mental health as we learn to think biblically.

In the process of rehabilitation, recognition is the first step. To uncover wrong expectations, we reviewed the most common ones in a variety of situations throughout many chapters of this book. Chapter 4 discussed the discernment of expectations through emotions, thoughts, and speech. Developing self-awareness that identifies specific emotions and thoughts, as well as listening to our words, is crucial. If we share our lives with other people, they may notice high expectations in our thoughts and hearts in areas where we are deceived or ignorant. Finally, God's Word and the Holy Spirit help identify our wrong thinking. Once these ways of thinking are exposed, rehabilitation may begin.

When we capture wrong thinking, we then align our thoughts with the truth God has revealed in his Word. If we learn, consider, and apply the implications of this truth to the specific expectations we have held, change in our thinking can occur. Specific tools to facilitate this process of rehabilitation will be discussed in more detail.

Self-Talk

We might engage in self-talk, not only for discerning thoughts and emotions but also for applying truth to the not-so-great expectations. In his book, *Spiritual Depression*, Dr. Martin Lloyd-Jones prescribes this treatment. "Very briefly at this point, the first thing we have to learn is what the Psalmist learned—we must learn to take ourselves in hand." He explains. "The main art in the matter of spiritual living is to know how to handle yourself. You have to take yourself in hand, you have to address yourself, preach to yourself, question yourself. You must say to your soul: 'Why art thou cast down—what business have you to be disquieted?'" [38]

While avoiding the very real problem, for some temperaments, of morbid over-introspection, many must stop and ask this question:

are my emotions uncovering an expectation of someone or some-thing? A previous expectation that other motorists will drive per-fectly was revised through self-talk. Why am I upset? Did I expect the other driver to never make an error?

How do we begin to talk sense to ourselves, to reorient our per-spective to God's truth? Two general practices of thought are helpful: think graciously and think godly. Gracious thoughts include con-sidering the other person and their point of view before your own, giving the benefit of the doubt, and trying to imitate God's kind-ness toward that person. Graciousness implements the Golden Rule found in in Matthew 7:12: "So in everything, do to others what you would have them do to you." We need grace not only from God but also from others, and we must become grace-givers like God. To think graciously also means to question the legitimacy of our own thoughts. In biblical terms, this resembles "log-looking," as prescribed in Matthew 7. When driving, as well as during any other activity, we must remember that we make mistakes and desire to be treated with forbearance.

To think godly means to search God's Word for biblical prin-ciples or examples that apply. The doctrine of the fall of humans implies that no one will perform perfectly all the time. Perfection is always too high of an expectation to have for other mortals.

After purchasing an item at a retail store, I walked away feeling angry toward the clerk for what I had perceived as rudeness. I enter-tained thoughts of not buying another item at that store (my feeble and inconsequential attempt at revenge). Later, I complained to my husband, who shares my expectations for pleasant customer ser-vice, and he began to negatively describe an experience he recently had with poor customer service. Now, both of us were wallowing in the mire of grumbling and negativity, which became so loud that I heard it. I paused in my grumbling and wondered, *What am I feeling? I am annoyed, pure and simple,* came the answer. *Why?* I

135

thought through the transaction. The clerk was not friendly; she was not helpful and seemed annoyed by my questions. When I was a store clerk, I remembered instructions to treat the customer well. "Be as pleasant as possible. Try to help the customer. Our continued business depends on the goodwill of the customer." I realized the expectation of customer service in my early working years surfaced and boiled negative emotions inside of me, ruining my joy. I expected that *I* should be treated as *I* thought *I* should be treated. Some may argue that politeness or pleasantness in a store clerk is a legitimate expectation. Maybe an employer can expect that attitude in his employees and make it a condition of employment, but to demand others to treat me (notice the four *I*'s in one sentence) according to my desires is self-centered, when we should be grace-centered.

When I became aware that my expectation for polite customer service had been disappointed, I began (at least this time) to rehabilitate that expectation through more self-talk. I tried to think graciously by valuing the clerk and trying to understand her perspective. *Maybe she was not taught to be pleasant to customers. Maybe she was taught this but was experiencing an awful day. Maybe hard or horrible events are currently occurring in her life. Maybe how she treats a customer is the last thing she needs to worry about. Maybe she has real struggles with finances, family, or health. Maybe she is a sinner just like me and could not care less about her job or me at the moment. Maybe I should get over my expectations of her and talk to God on her behalf.* Once I identified my high expectation of the clerk, heart space opened to humbly consider her, the other person in this situation. I prayed to God for her and immediately felt peace. This example involved a minor incident of annoyance, but the challenge to think graciously and godly will not be a one-stop easy path in small or large matters. Since wrong thinking can be tenacious, we may need to coach ourselves often and repeatedly in various situations.

One time, my three-year-old granddaughter, Rylie, and I were playing at a park when she bolted toward the tire swing, upon which were three boys, spinning and laughing. Rylie stopped several feet away and looked longingly at the tire swing. I heard her say to herself, "Wait your turn, Rylie." Then a moment later, she said again, "Wait your turn, Rylie." She evidently needed to self-talk twice to strengthen her resolve to do the right thing. We too may need to repeatedly talk truth to ourselves.

God's Word

In the process of rehabilitating not-so-great expectations, knowledge of the Bible is essential. God's Word illustrates characters with wrong expectations; tells the truth about life, people, and God; and communicates principles and standards of behavior. "Show me your ways, O Lord, teach me your paths; guide me in your truth and teach me, for you are God my Savior, and my hope is in you all day long" (Ps. 25:4-5). His ways are not always our ways. For example, when an injustice has been committed against us, we might have the natural expectation of seeking revenge. Instead, God's Word tells us to look to him. "Do not take revenge, my friends, but leave room for God's wrath, for it is written: 'It is mine to avenge; I will repay,' says the Lord" (Rom. 12:19). This verse specifically eliminates revenge. The next verse counsels that we should feed our enemies. This is only one example in which God's perspective turns our natural inclinations upside down.

The Word also reveals God as the ultimate gracious and forbearing person. He created us, communicated to us, and sent his only Son to redeem us. He could legitimately expect and demand an obedient response from us, while righteously rejecting us when we ignore or rebel against him.

Throughout the Old Testament, God endured much rejection as he repeatedly attempted to woo and care for the Israelite people. He gave the Israelites a land and identity as his chosen people, and He even gave them wealth and power at various times. However, again and again, the Israelites rejected His overtures of love. They turned from him to erect and worship idols. Yet, God continued to rescue, persuade, and plead with them before, during, and after times of judgment. He hoped the other nations would accurately know him through his concern and care for the nation of Israel. God's patient, forgiving, and forbearing dealings with Israel over thousands of years are a model for how we should treat other people.

In the New Testament, Jesus taught, healed, cared for, and then literally died for humanity, while entrusting himself to God the Father. Paul loved people by teaching the truth about Jesus, but he often experienced hurt and rejection in return. Both Jesus and Paul modeled forgiveness toward the people who hurt them.

God's Word not only displays forgiveness and forbearance, but it also describes the truth about people. We are creatures who bear the image of God, yet we are also sinners. We are sinners until we are saved through faith by

An ongoing and deepening knowledge of God's Word is fundamental to the ability to revise wrong expectations.

the grace given to us at Christ's death on the Cross. After we trust in Christ, we are redeemed sinners who have become new creations, although we continue to sin. We slowly grow into our new identity as God's children and toward maturity. We experience many setbacks along the way. In a world fallen from its original design, we struggle to live together with other sinners.

Because it reveals true knowledge, the Bible clarifies legitimate expectations of God, people, and life. An ongoing and deepening knowledge of God's Word is fundamental to the ability to revise wrong expectations.

Thus, we need to be lifelong learners of God's Word and skilled at applying it. In every disappointment, we need to ask, "What does God's Word say about this? What is God's perspective? What scriptures apply to this situation? How does His Word, in all its breadth, counsel our thoughts?" In this way, our thoughts might begin to align with God's truth and change our not-so-great expectations.

Prayer

When unable to discern wrong thoughts, prayer is essential. Sadly, only after years of confusion over my angry response to my husband's help with laundry did the necessity to pray occur to me.

The omniscient God knows us better than we know ourselves. In Psalm 139, David celebrates God's deeply intimate and personal knowledge of him. When struggling to understand a conflict or our thoughts and emotions, it is especially important and entirely appropriate that we, like David, ask God, "Search me, O God and know my heart; test me and know my anxious thoughts. See if there is any offensive way in me and lead me in the way everlasting" (139:23-24). When I specifically prayed these words and asked God to help me understand my emotions about the laundry, he revealed a deep-rooted lie: I was valuable only when I successfully kept pace with the laundry. Until I recognized this silly, perfectionistic demand I had placed on myself, I could not begin to challenge my incorrect thinking, heal my hurt, and help fix this marital conflict. Only after seeing the lie could I apply the unalterable truth from Scripture about my identity—that my worth is not ever tied to performance, for I am always a beloved daughter of the King. Then I prayed again for God's help to remind me of this truth when I "fail" at laundry, or at life. In order to see and rehabilitate our expectations, we may need to persist in this kind of prayer for a long time. In his instructions concerning relationship, Jesus commands us to keep asking, seeking, and knocking (Matt. 7:7). The verb tenses of each of these words in Greek suggest continuous and repeated action. Our Good Father promises that he will give us answers and make them known to us when we persevere in prayer for understanding and conformity to his truth.

Community

Another essential resource that can help us to discern wrong expectations is close fellowship with other believers. If we are regularly and deeply involved with our Christian friends, they may recognize our high or incorrect expectations through our speech or actions. To take advantage of this means of correction, we must maintain relational closeness. We also must cultivate vulnerable hearts that are willing to ask for and welcome correction, as well as the ability to speak gently for another's good. The motivation for a heart to become open to correction may arise from the conviction of the damage that wrong expectations often cause and also the desire for help and healing for ourselves and fellow believers.

In the biblical example discussed in chapter 6, Naaman, the King of Aram's commander, held two expectations: that Elisha would personally cure him and that the cure would look different than Elisha's prescription to wash in the Jordan River. Naaman was blinded by his perceptions as to the method Elisha would use to heal. Perhaps while venting his emotions, Naaman exposed his expectations, enabling his servants to challenge his thoughts. His servants then helped him realize his expectations were unreasonable and would prevent him from a possible cure. They spoke for the good of their master, possibly at great risk to themselves (2 Kgs. 5:13).

Similar to Naaman's servants, we may be called to seek discernment from others as well as offer challenges to wrong thinking in our community of believers. If we believe the Bible's assessment that our hearts are deceitful, we need input to understand our hearts and minds—especially untrue or unreasonable expectations that are buried and undiscovered within us. It will be hard to hear from others that our long-held expectations or ideas are unwarranted, but in the light of God's truth, we can then present ourselves for healing, like Naaman did.

In the same example, Gehazi did not consult anyone or Elisha, his master and a proven prophet of God. Instead, he kept his thoughts and feelings of injustice to himself. Gehazi acted on his not-so-great expectation, then contracted leprosy. Might Gehazi have been spared the consequence of his wrong expectation if he had shared his thoughts and opened himself to critique? We cannot know the answer for sure, but the sores of leprosy on Gehazi's body paint a vivid picture of the possible damage from wrong expectations that remain uncorrected.

The Bible teaches us not only through examples like Naaman and Gehazi, but it also commands us to "correct, rebuke and encourage using the word with great patience and careful instruction" (2 Tim. 4:2). To humbly question and potentially expose wrong expectations is an expression of love for one another.

Communicate Expectations

Finally, some expectations can be legitimate, but require clear communication. In a traditional wedding ceremony, when the man and the woman communicate and promise fidelity to each other, they both may legitimately expect faithfulness in marriage. Yet, fallen humans do not always keep their promises, and married couples must take great care not only to nurture their marriage but to flee temptation and "make no provision for the flesh in regard to its lusts" (Rom. 13:14, NASB).

In family matters, a married couple should communicate expectations about finances, the division of labor, holidays, and a myriad of other matters. Parents might rightly provide clear direction for their children to help with chores and share consequences for failures. Adults may enter contracts with each other where expectations of both parties are conveyed. For example, our church offers optional ministry houses for college students. In these houses, the students agree to uphold certain expectations as to chores, finances, and involvement in fellowship. Similarly, an engaged couple will wisely attempt to discover and communicate expectations concerning the big issues of their future life together. A friend may express his desires for quick responses to text messages or some other parameter of their friendship. Precise communication is best, no matter what kind of relationship where the goal is to build a healthy bond through unity and understanding.

When communicating expectations, a spirit of humility, not demand, should permeate the conversation. Perhaps ask, "Would you be willing to meet this expectation?" The importance of clear and humble communication cannot be overemphasized. In addition to recognition and rehabilitation of not-so-great expectations, gracious communication will help solve many problems.

Good communication and more realistic expectations will produce less disappointment, more joy, and grace-filled relationships. Perhaps best of all, as we communicate our expectations well, we will become a little more God-centered with demonstrably great hope in him. But the ultimate solution lies not in ourselves, it is found only in God. After questioning himself about his discouragement and disappointment in Psalms 42 and 43, the Psalmist commands his soul to put his hope in God. We too must replace our not-so-great expectations with hope in God.

Chapter 22: Replace Expectations with Hope

> *Hope is a good thing, maybe the best of things.* — *Andy Dufresne in The Shawshank Redemption*

Hope, Generally

Biblical hope is the antidote for wrong expectations. How does hope differ from expectations?

Biblical hope diverges from the current cultural use of the term *hope*, which expresses a wistful desire for something good to happen. The school child squeals, "I hope it's going to snow tomorrow!" The adult desires a promotion. The infertile couple desperately yearns for a baby. These examples express a desire for an outcome that is uncertain due to limited or no control in these situations. In a few passages, the Bible employs the word *hope* in this uncertain manner. Paul pens to the Corinthian church, "I hope to spend some time with you if the Lord permits" (1 Cor. 16:7). To the church at Philippi, Paul wants to send Timothy to them "as soon as I see how things go with me" (Phil. 2:18, 23). More often in both the Old and New Testament, hope conveys a confident assurance when the object of hope is God.

A word study yielded ten Hebrew words translated as *hope*. One of the Old Testament words, *tiqvah,* literally means a cord, a line, or an attachment. This word was used in the literal sense in the story of Rahab found in Joshua chapter 2. In this story, Joshua sent two spies to Jericho, who came to the apartment of Rahab, a prostitute. After the king of Jericho suspected their location, he ordered Rahab to surrender the men. Rahab hid the spies on her roof and lied to the messengers of the king, indicating they had already left. Subsequently, Rahab explained to the Israelite spies why she was willing to take such a risk. She said, "We heard how the Lord dried up the water of the Red Sea for you when you came out of Egypt and what you did to Sihon and Og, the two kings of the Amorites east of the Jordan whom you completely destroyed. When we heard of it, our hearts melted and everyone's courage failed because of you, for the Lord your God is God in heaven above and on the earth below" (Josh. 2:10-11). Rahab expressed hope, not in the spies but in their God—in who he is and what he had done. In contrast to regional gods, which were plentiful during that period of history, Rahab acknowledged God's complete sovereignty over heaven and earth. She then asked the Israelites for protection in return for keeping their secret. The spies requested Rahab to hang a scarlet cord (*tiqvah*) in her window, which they would see upon return to the city. After they had left, she secured the scarlet cord as they had asked (Josh. 2:18, 21).

This word, *tiqvah,* provides a metaphorical picture that hope is like a cord. It is the rope upon which we hang, where we rest our weight. When we attach ourselves to God and what he has done for us, we are like Rahab. Hope in God resembles clinging to a strong cord. We hang onto him and nothing else. He is certain: a durable cord. Refusing to trust in the gods of Jericho or the king of Jericho,

Rahab hoped in the God of the spies alone. Later occurrences in the Old Testament translate *tiqvah* as hope.

A phrase that similarly expresses the idea of hope is found in Psalm 62:10, which counsels us not to *set our hearts* on riches. Where we set our heart echoes the idea of hanging our weight. Hope then involves a choice of our wills. The Psalmist often states, "I *will* hope in God." This same choice is before us as well. Will *we* hope in God; will we set our heart on him?

Interestingly, the word study also yielded the result that before the period of the kings in the Old Testament, very few uses of the word *hope* existed, except in Job, as well as the extremely rare usage of the word in the Gospels. One commentator speculated the scarcity of the word suggests hope is less necessary when God is more visibly present. Prior to Israel's kings, God directly ruled by way of theocracy and later through judges. In the Gospels, the word *hope* only appears three to five times until after the physical ascension of Jesus in Acts. After these periods, when God was less directly perceptible as King or less physically present through Jesus, hope becomes essential, and the word is more plentiful.

Like the believers who lived after the directly visible presence of God in Christ, we also need hope. We have the advantage of God's Spirit dwelling within us, and he helps us see God. He convicts, reminds, and prompts us to set anew our hearts on God. He helps us to hope.

Hope may be confused with faith, which is similar. Both involve the idea of trust, but faith stresses rational belief or evidence, which gives rise to trust. Faith begins in the mind, whereas hope accentuates the heart. Faith is a necessary precondition for real hope, which needs evidence. For schoolchildren in Key West, Florida, the hope for a snow day has little evidence to support it. Our hearts cannot truly hope in what we know is false or highly uncertain. Faith fills out the cord on which we are hanging, whether it is as thin as spider's silk or as thick as a robust cable. Rahab evaluated the evidence concerning what God had done: parting the Red Sea and conquering the cities of Sihon and Og. Based on this evidence, Rahab believed in the God of Israel, acknowledging his sovereignty over the entire heaven and earth. She then chose to hang her hope on God and his agents. The author of Hebrews expresses this connection between faith and hope. "Faith shows the reality of what we hope for; it is the evidence of things we cannot see" (Heb. 11:1, NLT). Hope then is dependent on evidence-based faith.

Faith is also distinguished from hope in that faith is primarily oriented to the present, what we believe and trust in now. Hope is generally future and forward-looking. When we hope, we are trusting that our present faith will deliver in the future. "Who hopes for what he already has? But if we hope for what we do not yet have, we wait for it patiently" (Rom. 8:24-25). Hope in its future orientation often requires waiting, but it is not passive. We watch while we wait, searching for God during this process. We look for signs of God at work according to our knowledge of his past trustworthiness. "I wait for the Lord, my soul waits, and in his word, I put my hope. My soul waits for the Lord more than watchmen wait for the morning" (Ps. 130:5-6).

For more than two years, our small group hoped and prayed for a member of our group to obtain a higher-paying job so his wife could stay home with their son. We envisioned a promotion in the large corporation where he currently worked. Eventually, on the miscellaneous email of our church, a position in an automotive repair shop appeared, which fit this man's burden to serve others by repairing cars. He was awarded the position. Our small group collectively rejoiced and marveled at God's answer, which came in his perfect but unexpected way. "Now to him who is able to do immeasurably more than all we ask or imagine, according to his power that is at work within us ..." (Eph. 3:20). However, it was hard for our friend to wait for a different job, as the waiting process in any difficult circumstance can be hard.

Finally, hope has an emotional component that is different than faith. When we set our hearts on God, we experience less disappointment because God does not disappoint. When hope is fulfilled, we experience great joy. Peace, which is a fruit of the Holy Spirit, is also an indication and the result of resting our hearts on God. If our hearts are continually frantic, we are not at rest. "Let all that I am wait quietly before God, for my hope is in him" (Ps. 62:5, NLT).

How is hope different from expectation, and why is it better? With not-so-great expectations, we look to people or life to give us what only God can. We are setting our hearts on God's good gifts and blessings, rather than him alone. This is idolatry, which will lead to disappointment. Jeremiah wisely asks, "Do any of the worthless idols of the nations bring rain? Do the skies themselves send down showers? No, it is you, O Lord our God. Therefore our hope is in you, for you are the one who does all this" (Jer. 14:22). Yet, our natural tendencies incline us to rely on self, others, or circumstances, rather than God.

Unlike expectations that exalt our perspective, biblical hope is humble. "My heart is not proud, Lord, my eyes are not haughty. I do not concern myself with great matters or things too wonderful for me. But I have calmed and quieted myself, like a weaned child with its mother; like a weaned child I am content. Israel put your hope in the Lord both now and forevermore" (Ps. 131:1-3). In this passage, the Psalmist connects humility with the willing surrender of understanding life beyond our ability. When we demand anything from God, people, or life, we imply we know better than those from whom we are demanding. Hope admits some knowledge is beyond our understanding but not beyond God's.

Hope is the answer to the insignificance and brevity of our lives, while expectations house small ideas in that they concern earthly and temporal people or circumstances. A conversation with my daughter reminded me of this distinction. Attempting to locate Aruba on a map where my sister was vacationing, we noticed the vast distance from home. We discussed how small our city was compared to all the world, our earth, a speck in the universe. I sighed and said to my daughter, "But for God and my relationship with him, I would despair at my insignificance." When we honestly contemplate the triviality of any created thing compared to God, we are driven to him, acknowledging that he is our only hope. "Man is a mere phantom as he goes to and fro: He bustles about, but only in vain; he heaps up wealth, not knowing who will get it. But now, Lord, what do I look for? My hope is in you" (Ps. 39:6-7). For followers of Jesus Christ, hope in God and his truth is the ultimate answer for unmet or unwarranted expectations of people or life. A chart summarizing the differences between not-so-great expectations and hope follows.

	Not So Great Expectations	Hope
Attitude	Expresses unwarranted certainties and seems right: "We know"	Suspicious of our view and holds our perspective humbly
Choice in response to feelings	Desires but then chooses to place demands in relationships	Desires but clings and entrusts self to God without any demand of him or others

Focus	Horizontal: Looking to sinful, frail people or temporal circumstances	Vertical: Looking to who God is and what he has done
Source	Based on our thoughts and perceptions	Based on God's truth
Worship	Often makes idols of people or life	God is on the throne of our hearts
Time	Want it now	Often involves waiting on God
Outcome	Disappointment in self, people and life circumstances Destructive to relationships and joy	Hope says, "But God" Gracious: Gives out of the wealth received from God Grateful: Rejoices in God and every spiritual blessing

In case it might help to add clarity to the process of replacing wrong expectations with hope, I offer this practical example from my own life. While completing this book, my husband's sales agency was threatened when a competitor tried to hijack his primary product line. The livelihood we had enjoyed for twenty years appeared to be at an end. We had expected his business would continue until retirement, and I was unemployed. Now, hope in God was not a theory. Would we practice these words and hope in God? We knew we could not put hope in anything or anyone other than God. "A horse is a vain hope" (Ps. 33:17). We knew not to trust in wealth, even the wealth of a job. But our trembling anxiety and excessive discouragement revealed we did not know this truth in our hearts; indeed, we had hoped in these things. We struggled to hope in God, and the question arose: what practical steps encourage hope in God?

Prayer

Upon learning the news, talking with our Father became the priority. We prayed, both separately and together, expressing our emotions to God. We were sad and fearful. The home business had enabled our family to enjoy great flexibility in addition to sufficient income. We thanked God for many years of blessing. I was specifically grateful for the timing of the difficult prospect, since I was steeped in God's Word, studying why and how we can hope in him. We also prayed for protection, since the changes seemed motivated by evil intent and greed.

Understandably, my husband experienced personal hurt from the apparent disregard of years of investment and loyalty to this manufacturer. He admitted his desire for revenge by recruiting sympathetic customers to turn against the manufacturer. I began to pray specifically that God would help my husband not pursue vengeful actions.

Without a word from me, God communicated to my husband that he should not take matters into his own hands but instead choose to wait for God. I experienced an answer to prayer and celebrated God's mindfulness of us, which fortified further faith and hope. Is it not like our God to encourage us along the way? Yet, we had to continue to wait.

Wait and Watch

When hoping in God, waiting cannot be avoided. He does not move according to our desired time frames. However, waiting is not passive. We are to be watchful in our waiting. Watchful waiting requires searching for God's involvement and direction in our lives. It involves an active evaluation of choices that are in line with God's truth. "We do not know what to do, but our eyes are upon you" (2

Chron. 20:12). Active waiting involves continual reading of God's Word and seeking help from his community.

Community

During this time, our community of believers was a great blessing. We shared with them the events and why we were concerned. Although sharing exposed our vulnerability, it also lifted some of our burdens. In our weekly prayer time together, some of them would often pray with confidence and power, strengthening our hearts to persevere. Our friends expressed concern and offered help, allowing us to talk with them and process our emotions and fears. Our fellow believers became a direct conduit of God's love and strength, as they also helped us to continue to pursue God's ways.

Act with Integrity

As we continued to pray and wait, we knew that hoping in God meant that our actions must have integrity or, in other words, be consistent with God's ways. Specifically, God's Spirit led my husband not to seek vengeance; rather, God's grace called him past revenge to pray for the competitor. *Oh yes, pray for our enemies. I have heard that somewhere,* I thought.

In addition to prayer for direction, my husband sought guidance from trustworthy people in his industry but always weighed their advice against God's Word. Several offered to help my husband secure a competing product line. While the support was comforting, to proceed in this way seemed premature and disloyal, until he was terminated through the industry-standard thirty-day notice. To walk in integrity meant to continue waiting. We pursued the activities God would have us do anyway. My husband worked hard at his job as unto the Lord. During this time, we stayed engaged in the community of believers and spiritual work. "Yes, LORD, walking in the way of your laws, we wait for you; your name and renown are the desire of our hearts (Isa. 26:8).

Remember God's Faithfulness

Finally, we scheduled a time for the sole purpose to remember God's faithfulness. We recalled specific instances in the past where God had protected the business. We remembered countless times when God provided for us in financial matters. Since my husband earned commission, the business income sometimes widely fluctuated. But God repeatedly met our needs in unique ways according to his perfect time and often in precise detail.

Remembering God's faithfulness is of prime importance for discarding wrong expectations and hoping in him. When we know God has noticed and provided for us, joy overflows within us, and peace grows through experiences of his sovereign care. In great despair, the Psalmist writes, "To this I will appeal: the years when the Most High stretched out his right hand. I will remember the deeds of the Lord; yes, I will remember your miracles of long ago. I will consider all your works and meditate on all your mighty deeds" (Ps. 77:10-12). When we recall God's faithfulness, it helps to hope in him today and for tomorrow. And so it did. A chronicle of God's individual and special care builds our personal treasured book of hope.

Finally, we remembered and consciously recalled big-perspective truth. God reminded us that our lives are more than our circumstances. Our lives are unstoppably moving to a glorious future, no matter the obstacles. After working through and sometimes repeating these many steps, we consciously set our hearts on him.

Years later, my husband still has the business and supporting product line. Through that experience, God taught us to loosen our grip a little more on a job or other earthly and temporary circumstances.

The ability to replace not-so-great expectations with hope in God is and will always be greatly aided by true contentment concerning who God is and what he has done and promised. So much could be said and celebrated about our triune God, too much to be contained in any book. "If every one of them were written down, I suppose that even the whole world would not have room for the books that would be written" (John 21:25). Nevertheless, these final chapters attempt to provide a summary reminder of the reasons why hope in God makes perfect and everlasting sense.

Our lives are unstoppably moving to a glorious future, no matter the obstacles.

Chapter 23:
Hope in God

Find rest O my soul in God alone; my hope comes from him. He alone is my rock and my salvation; he is my fortress, I will not be shaken (Ps. 62:5-6).

Hope in God surpasses any expectation in any created person or earthly circumstance. His Word reveals abundant information about God that persuades us to replace our not-so-great expectations with hope in him.

Hope in God's Word

Through his Word, God reveals his attributes and character, and he demonstrates his actions throughout history. God's Word then is a foundational source to grow hope. "I wait for the Lord, my soul waits, and in his word, I put my hope" (Ps. 130:5). Apart from his spoken Word, we cannot know specific ideas about God and what he has done. As we view creation, we can know of his power, majesty, and love for beauty and variety, but we cannot know his thoughts or truth about people and life. God gave his Word so we would have hope. "For everything that was written in the past was written to teach us, so that through endurance and the encouragement of the Scriptures we might have hope" (Rom. 15:4).

The interaction between faith and hope can again be seen in this context. Behind hope in God's Word, there must be confidence or faith in the Bible as truth. For hope to be sure, we must believe we are reading revelation from God. Many resources comprehensively address the Bible's historical reliability, its unity, its integrity, and the substantial evidence that it is a supernatural book. It is a necessary endeavor for each Christian to build convictions concerning God's Word. This discussion, however, is beyond the scope of this book.[39] While difficult issues and passages are present in both the Old and New Testaments, the vast majority of God's Word is clear, helpful, and beautiful. When we are convinced of its veracity, we will be like the Psalmist in Psalm 119, able to truly hope in God's Word, as he writes, "I have put my hope in your word" (vv. 43, 74, 81, 114, 147). We will then confidently look to God's Word and put our hope in what it expresses about who God is and what he has done.

Hope in Who God Is

In chapter 7, we surveyed wrong expectations of God: that he is our genie or a taker, that he owes us a good life or a specific revelation, and that he is powerless or unwilling. God's attributes and character answer our wrong ideas. Far from disappointing us, God is the God of hope, as Paul calls him: "May the God of hope fill you with all joy and peace as you trust in him, so that you may overflow with hope by the power of the Holy Spirit" (Rom. 15:13). As we gaze upon God and his works, he imparts hope to us through the power of the Holy Spirit. What knowledge of God helps us to hope in him?

God Is Loving and Good

Some of our wrong expectations question God's goodness and love. Early in my relationship with God, this lie was exposed in my heart. I once believed God was limited in goodness, not infinite in goodness, thinking his goodness would end. I had confused a legitimate expectation that hardships might occur due to sin and a fallen world with a limitation on God's goodness. To rehabilitate these thoughts, I recalled specific truth about God's goodness.

God proclaimed his name to Moses. "The Lord, the Lord, the compassionate and gracious God, slow to anger, abounding in love and faithfulness, maintaining love to thousands and forgiving wickedness, rebellion and sin" (Exod. 34:6-7). God abounds in love and *maintains* his love for thousands. The Psalms also declare God's unending goodness and love. "For the Lord is good and his love endures forever; his faithfulness continues through all generations" (100:5). The Bible paints God's unlimited goodness in many ways and dispels the lie that his goodness will end. Even if life becomes difficult, God has not ceased to be good and loving.

We can hope in God because God *is* love (1 John 4:8). Not only is God the essence of love, but he has defined and demonstrated his perfect love in sending his Son to die in our place. When we are tempted to believe God is not good or does not care, we need only to look at the Cross. In contrast to anything or anyone in this life, no human person loves or can love to this extent. Recalling truth and replacing wrong thinking is not a one-time event; it is an ongoing, repeated process we must undertake every time we distrust and doubt God's goodness and love.

God Is a Giver

The belief that God wants to take or rob me of a good life is refuted by God's description of himself and a quick survey of his blessings. In the Bible, God compares himself to a good human father who delights to give good gifts to his children (Matt. 7:11). What are some of those good gifts from God, our Father?

God does not give what we deserve: judgment, wrath, death, and separation from him. Instead, he grants us a plethora of blessings that we do not deserve: forgiveness, power, and purpose. He *adopts* us. Concerning this adoption, John exclaims, "How great is the love the Father has lavished on us, that we should be called children of God!"(1 John 3:1). He gives us himself in the Holy Spirit, who helps us know and experience him intimately (Rom. 5:5). We are free to ask for anything and everything because the Bible tells us he *longs to be gracious* to us at the right time (Isa. 30:18). Because God does not desire to take or withhold any good thing but instead is eager to give, we can anchor hope in him.

Not only is hope in God logical, but it will be rewarded. "The LORD is good to those whose hope is in him, to the one who seeks him" (Lam. 3:25). We who hope in God will not be disappointed (Isa. 49:23), nor put to shame (Ps. 25:3). We will have our strength renewed (Isa. 40:31). Despite circumstances or perceptions, God is always and forever a giver in who we can hope.

God Is Faithful

We can hope in God because he is faithful. The author of Lamentations admits his suffering and bitterness at the fall of Jerusalem and the exile of his people, but then he changes his focus to God's faithfulness, which gives him hope. He says, "Yet this I call to mind and therefore I have hope: Because of the Lord's great love, we are not consumed, for his compassions never fail. They are new every morning: great is your faithfulness" (Lam. 3:21-23). Despite our perception of circumstances or feelings of abandonment, God is faithful daily.

God Is Powerful

Scripture answers the low expectation that God lacks power, which is often manifested by a failure to pray. *El Shaddai* is a Hebrew name for God which means God Almighty or God the All-Powerful One (Gen. 17:1; 49:25). God performed supernatural acts in part so humans would know his power and rightly revere him. In the Old Testament, God parted the Jordan River and the Red Sea. "He did this so that all the peoples of the earth might know that the hand of the Lord is powerful and so that you might always fear the Lord your God" (Josh. 4:24). Jesus also performed miracles that healed, liberated, and restored people. He demonstrated power over the weather and even over death. Power without love is frightening, but the God of the Bible is both. "One thing God has spoken, two things I have heard: 'Power belongs to you, God, and with you, Lord, is unfailing love'" (Ps. 62:11–12a). God's power is always exercised for our good.

God Is Near and Not Silent

Concerning the demand that God reveal himself, discussed in chapter 7, we hope in the fact that God has already spoken and that he continues to speak to us through his Word, through creation (Ps. 19:1–4), through his Son (Heb. 1:2), and through the Holy Spirit (Jn. 14:26).

God's communication repeatedly emphasizes his constant nearness. "He will never leave you nor forsake you" (Deut. 31:6; Heb.

13:5). "And surely I am with you always to the very end of the age" (Matt. 28:20). "He is not far from each one of us" (Acts 17:27). When we feel alone in a loveless marriage, hurt by a friend, or unnoticed at work, or if we think that God is aloof and distant, we recall these truths. We can celebrate with Hagar, Sarah's maid who bore Abraham's son, Ishmael. When she ran away after being mistreated, an angel of the Lord came to her. She was amazed that God had paid attention to her, a mere servant. "She gave this name to the Lord who spoke to her: You are the God who sees me, for she said, I have now seen the One who sees me" (Gen. 16:13). God sees us! We need his help to open our eyes to see him seeing us.

We also need God's help to appreciate the wondrous nobility of his nearness and attention. The movie *Hidden Figures*[40] provides a weak analogy. John Glenn, the famous astronaut and later statesman, deliberately and against his advisors went out of his way to acknowledge and appreciate the undervalued and mistreated black women who performed the calculations that enabled him to safely travel and return from his space mission. He dignified and elevated their status to the world with his attention. Similarly, any attention from the majestic and all-mighty God dignifies and magnifies us. Hagar experienced this wonder, and we will sometimes experience the wonder of God's nearness and care in our own lives. But such attention is not ours to demand.

We have looked at a few characteristics throughout the Bible that describe God. Psalm 145 provides a wonderful example to meditate on God. In an attempt to adequately describe God, David used many evocative words: King, unfathomable greatness, abundant goodness, righteous, gracious, compassionate, slow to anger, rich in love, trustworthy, faithful, and near. David culminated his description of God and said each generation will speak of the "glorious splendor of his majesty" (145:5). This phrase repeats synonyms of magnificence to help us appreciate God. David seemingly wrestled with words to expand our understanding of God. Each of these descriptive words unseals the possibility for deep meditation about God. Beyond David's descriptions in Psalm 145, all of the characteristics of God provide hope and answer not-so-great expectations. God is unlike any human person. He is worthy of hope not only because of who he is, but also because of his works.

Chapter 24:
Hope in God's Actions

But the Lord Almighty will be exalted by his justice and the holy God will be proved holy by his righteous acts (Isa. 5:16).

God proves he is a secure hope by his actions throughout history. From the beginning, God initiated a relationship with his creatures. In the garden, he walked with Adam and Eve. After their rebellion, he covered their nakedness. He chose Abraham and his descendants to be his special people through which he would work. God gave the Israelites an identity, a land, and a purpose. He bestowed upon them blessings, freed them from slavery, fought for them, and forgave them. He sent judges to help them and prophets to warn them. In exile and after discipline, he still pursued them. He returned them to their land and rebuilt their temple. Throughout these transactions, God intertwined promises for a Redeemer, not only to Israel, but to all the nations.

After four hundred years without a prophet, God sent the last prophet, the ultimate Deliverer, his promised Messiah, his only Son. The linchpin of human history occurred when God entered the human race by the power of the Holy Spirit through the womb of a young maiden. The Old Testament long foreshadowed and foretold his coming.[41] For three years, Jesus healed, taught, and corrected misunderstandings about God and his plan.

In the definitive act of love, Jesus, God incarnate, willingly died on the Cross to rescue Israel and all people. "You were redeemed … with the precious blood of Christ, a lamb without blemish or defect. He was chosen before the creation of the world but was revealed in these last times for your sake. Through him, you believe in God who raised him from the dead and glorified him and so your faith and hope are in God" (1 Pet. 1:18-21). This act of God, above all else, is why we can have bold and unwavering hope in him.

From a limited human perspective, the Cross would have appeared as the worst possible scenario. God's innocent, anointed Son hung dying naked on a tree. Yet, through this act, God accomplished his greatest good: a way of escape for deservedly doomed humans. When life seemingly spins out of control, we can hope most of all in the Cross of Jesus.

The resurrection of Jesus proves that God accepted the sacrifice of Jesus and also provides tangible hope for our resurrection after death. "Praise be to the God and Father of our Lord Jesus Christ. In his great mercy, he has given us new birth into a living hope through the resurrection of Jesus Christ from the dead and into an inheritance that can never perish, spoil or fade—kept in heaven for you" (1 Pet. 1:3-4).

After Jesus's resurrection, our loving Father bestowed the gift of the Holy Spirit. Jesus promised, "I will not leave you as orphans" (John 14:18). "The Father … will give you another Counselor to be with you forever—the Spirit of truth" (John 14:16-17). The apostles were distraught at the prospect of Jesus leaving. His departure made no sense to them, for their expectations looked different than the plan of God. "Because I have said these things, you are filled with grief. But I tell you the truth: It is for your good that I am going away. Unless I go away, the Counselor will not come to you" (John

16:6-7). The apostles waited fifty days for the promise of the Holy Spirit to be fulfilled.

Like the apostles, we possess a limited perspective, as many of God's actions or inactions sometimes do not make sense to us. Our expectations also look different than the plan of God. We often must wait for understanding or his promises to be fulfilled, some of which may not occur in our lifetimes. From our privileged position in history, hindsight proves that God does make sense, and His plans and ways are always supremely good; far better than we can imagine.

God acted, Jesus acted, and the Holy Spirit continues to act on our behalf. A condensed history of God's works convinces us there is no better hope than in the Triune God. "You answer us with awesome deeds of righteousness, O God our Savior, the hope of all the ends of the earth and of the farthest seas" (Ps. 65:5).

> *From our privileged position in history, hindsight proves that God does make sense, and His plans and ways are always supremely good; far better than we can imagine.*

Chapter 25:
Hope in God's Promises

Remember your promise to me; it is my only hope (Ps. 119:49, NLT).

God, his essence and actions, anchors our soul and corrects our wrong expectations. His promises offer us more reason to hope. Unlike human promises, which may be well-intentioned, God's promises are certain; they are entirely trustworthy. Based on God's character, we have every reason to expect he will keep his promises. In Numbers 23:19, the prophet Balaam states, "God is not human, that he should lie, not a human being, that he should change his mind. Does he speak and then not act? Does he promise and not fulfill?"

History also teaches us that God has kept his promises. We know he kept his promise to Abraham to make his descendants numerous. God also kept his promises to Israel, both for the original possession of their land and their return from exile. Though enslaved in Egypt for four hundred years, Israel eventually received their land and freedom. After much of the land was settled, Joshua acknowledged, "Not one of all the Lord's good promises to the house of Israel failed; every one was fulfilled" (21:45).

God promised the exiled Israelites in Babylon they would return, despite the many years they disregarded his warnings. "This is what the Lord says: 'When seventy years are completed for Babylon, I will come to you and fulfill my gracious promise to bring you back to this place. For I know the plans I have for you,' declares the Lord, 'plans to prosper you and not to harm you, plans to give you hope and a future'" (Jer. 29:10–11). The exiles returned and rebuilt the temple in Jerusalem.

God will keep his promises to us. "Let us hold tightly without wavering to the hope we affirm, for God can be trusted to keep his promise." (Heb. 10:23, NLT). What are some of these promises?

God's presence is specifically and repeatedly promised. A good friend remembered a time of loneliness after a move to work in a small town away from family and friends. Though new in her relationship with God, she cried to him, telling him she felt desperately alone. She believed God responded, "It is okay to feel lonely but not to feel alone because you are never alone. I am always with you." This treasured personal experience, confirmed by the promise of Scripture, helped her to hope in God in that time of isolation.

The promises of God can help us confront high expectations in our ability to change persistent sin habits, as examined in chapter 10. Hope for transformation is found in God's commitment, not our strength to change. "It is God's will that you should be sanctified" (1 Thess. 4:3). Sanctification simply describes the process of spiritual growth, the transformation of our former selves into the image of the only perfect human, Jesus Christ. Although Ezekiel addressed the nation of Israel, God's promise to transform may be extended to us. "And I will put my Spirit in you and

We can be certain God will keep his promises but must guard our expectations as to how and when he will fulfill them.

165

move you to follow my decrees and be careful to keep my laws" (Ezek. 36:25-27). Multiple times in the Ezekiel passage, God promises that he will perform the heavy lifting of renewal.

God also promises to bring good from all things, including suffering. "And we know that in all things God works for the good of those who love him, who have been called according to his purpose" (Rom. 8:28). After Paul recounts great suffering in Asia, he explains one good outcome: "That we might not rely on ourselves but on God who raises from the dead" (2 Cor. 1:9). Increased dependence on God often happens through suffering.

Also, only in great peril do we sense our need and experience the goodness of God's rescue, which then produces hope for the future. "On him we have set our hope that he will continue to deliver us" (2 Cor. 1:10). We can be certain God will keep his promises to us, but we must guard our expectations as to *how* and *when* he will fulfill them.

Great hope not only rests in God's faithfulness and fulfillment of past promises but also generates faith for promises concerning our future eternity. "If only for this life we have hope in Christ, we are of all people most to be pitied" (1 Cor. 15:19). Perhaps our greatest hope is in the promise of life to come.

Hope in the Promise of Eternity

Finally, God promises a perfect and eternal life with him. We have "the hope of eternal life, which God who does not lie, promised before the beginning of time" (Titus 1:2). In God, not-so-great expectations will be mended. God will expose all our wrong and disappointed expectations and replace them with the fullness of himself and his truth. Perfect justice will be achieved. When injustice multiplies and when those who abhor or ignore God seem to prosper, we can hope. "Do not let your heart envy sinners, but always be zealous for the fear of the Lord. There is surely a future hope for you and your hope will not be cut off" (Prov. 23:17-18).

Death for the believer will be "swallowed up in victory" (1 Cor. 15:54). God will revise our dim misconceptions of him with the overwhelming glory of his perfect love and never-ending majesty. All the struggles with our humanity, our physical frailty, and sinfulness will be replaced with new, everlasting glorified bodies and beautiful love relationships. Our loneliness and life disappointments will be absorbed in the triumph of new life, the hope of a new heaven and earth. "And I heard a loud voice from the throne saying, Look! God's dwelling place is now among the people, and he will dwell with them. They will be his people, and God himself will be with them and be their God. He will wipe every tear from their eyes. There will be no more death or mourning or crying or pain, for the old order of things has passed away" (Rev. 21:3-4).

The end of human history will coincide with Christ's return; "while we wait for the blessed hope—the glorious appearing of our great God and Savior, Jesus Christ" (Titus 2:13). This hope is not pie-in-the-sky wishful thinking, nor the opiate of the masses or the drug of the deluded. This future hope of eternal life is based on thousands of years of completed and written history of promises proven true. It is also rooted in each individual's cumulated lifetime experience of God's personal faithfulness. This hope is certain now but will be unnecessary after death. Hope will be fully and finally consummated in the wonderful reality of our eternal home with our Father God.

Conclusion

For all who hope in God, we will be continually challenged to cling only to him. When we stake our lives on him, we make a sure bet. In the final and forever analysis, those who entrust themselves to God will not be disappointed. We will also experience much joy and blessing in this life to the extent we hope in God. It has been said that "joy is the infallible sign of the presence of God."[42] Perhaps as we hope in God, our joy will also bring his presence a little nearer to this hurting world.

> *"Be strong and take heart all you who hope in the Lord"*
> *(Ps. 31:24).*

Endnotes

1   Phillip Yancey, *Disappointment with God* (Grand Rapids: Zondervan, 1988) concerns expectations of God. Paul Tripp, *What Did You Expect? Redeeming the Realities of Marriage* (Wheaton, IL: Crossway, 2010) concerns expectations in marriage. Many parenting books mention expectations. One example is: Walter Henrichsen, *How to Disciple your Children* (Wheaton, IL: Victor Books, 1978).

2   Merriam Webster's Collegiate Dictionary, 11th ed. (2008), s.v. "expect."

3   *An Expository Dictionary of Biblical Words,* W.E. Vine, Merrill Unger, William White, Jr, (Nashville: Thomas Nelson, 1985) s.v. "expect, expectation."

4   In *A Case for Faith,* Video Interview with Lee Stroebel, Sept 11, 2013, https://www.youtube.com/watch?v=5qCvWj8rNv0.

5   Bruce Wilkinson, *Seven Laws of the Learner,* (Atlanta: Multnomah Books, 1992), 88–105.

6   A ministry house is an example where promises are made such as to share living expenses and household responsibilities in addition to helping each other grow in their relationship with Jesus. See for example: https://www.xenos.org/college/ministry-house-agreement.

7   All Scripture quotations are from *Holy Bible, New International Version* (NIV) (Grand Rapids: Zondervan, 1984, 2011) unless otherwise noted.

8   Suggestions for doing this are to ask a person in your life who avidly studies the Bible or you sense has a qualitatively different relationship with God. You may contact www.xenos.org for teaching resources where you will repeatedly hear this message or contact the author. As I write this, I pray for the reader to have a heart to seek God truly, humbly and diligently. See Deut. 4:29 and Proverbs 8:17 for just two of the many places where God promises if we seek him we will find him.

9   *An Expository Dictionary of Biblical Words,* W.E. Vine, Merrill Unger, William White, Jr, (Nashville: Thomas Nelson, 1985) s.v. "expect, expectation."

10   Michael J. Fox Interview with ABC's Diane Sawyer: *Good Morning America,* ABC News, May 6, 2009: http://abcnews.go.com/GMA/story id=7511362.

11   *All's Well That Ends Well,* Act II, scene 1, line 125: https://www.playshakespeare.com/alls-well-that-ends-well/scenes/act-ii-scene-1

12   This story is recounted in, V. Phillips Long, *The Art of Biblical History, Volume 5.* (Zondervan: Grand Rapids, 1994), 31–32.

13   Gerard Prendergast, Leung Kwok Yan, & Douglas C. West, "Role Portrayal in Advertising and Editorial Content and Eating Disorders: An Asian Perspective" *International Journal of Advertising: The Review of Marketing Communication.* Volume 21, Issue 2, 2002, 237–258.

14   See for example the discussion in: J. Julius Scott, *Jewish Backgrounds to the New Testament,* (Grand Rapids: Baker Books, 1995,2000), 307-324

15   (New York: Penguin Books, 2013), 98.

16   Phillip Yancey (Grand Rapids: Zondervan, 1988.)

17   Yancey, 32.

18   From a sermon given by William Carey on May 30, 1792.

19   Robert B. Chisolm, Jr., *Interpreting the Historical Books: An Exegetical Handbook* (Grand Rapids: Kregel, 2006), 94.

20   Term used by Francis Schaeffer in *True Spirituality*, (Wheaton: Tyndale House Publishers, 1971, 2001).

21   C.S. Lewis, *Mere Christianity*, (New York: HarperCollins, 2001). 226 and Timothy Keller, *The Freedom of Self Forgetfulness* (Leyland, England: 10Publishing, 2012).

22   Institutes, 1.1.1. https://reformed.org/books/institutes/books/book1/bk1ch01.html, accessed May 15,2020.

23   See Ephesians 6: 10–18 where Paul delineates the full armor of God as provision for the battle.

24   (Ventura: Regal Books, 1990), 181-192.

25   Edward Welch, *Side by Side: Walking with others in Wisdom and Love* (Wheaton: Crossway, 2015), 133-139.

26   Timothy Keller, *The Meaning of Marriage* (New York: Penguin, 2011), 70.

27   Ajieth Fernando, *Reclaiming Love* (Grand Rapids: Zoondervan, 2012), 26.

28   Dennis McCallum and Jessica Lowery, *Organic Discipleship*, (Columbus: New Paradigm Publishing, 2012), 137.

29   Paul Tripp, (Wheaton: Crossway, 2010), 32.

30   *Jerry Maguire*, directed by Cameron Crowe, performed by Tom Cruise and Renee Zellweger, (1996, TriStar Pictures, Sony Pictures Entertainment), Film.

31   *This Is Where I Leave You*; *August: Osage County*, *The Royal Tennebaums*; *Running with Scissors; Little Miss Sunshine; Garden State; Home for the Holidays* are just a few in recent years.

32   (Grand Rapids: Baker Books, 1975), 64-68.

33 C. Hassell Bullock, *An Introduction to the Old Testament Poetic Books*, (Chicago: Moody Publishers, 1988), 192.

34 I could not find the book I read in the 1990s. This is not the same title as the 2005 book of the same name, *How to Lead Your Child to Christ* by Robert and Bobbie Wolgemuth, (Colorado Springs: Focus on the Family Publishing).

35 Ray Comfort, (Bartlesville: Genesis Publishing Group, 2005).

36 D.A. Carson, *For the Love of God*, Volume One, (Wheaton: Crossway Books, 1998), January 10.

37 Possibly in a Letter to Fortescue (1725).

38 D. Martyn Lloyd-Jones, *Spiritual Depression, Its Causes and Cure*, (Grand Rapids: Eerdmans Publishing, 1965), 20-21.

39 See for example, K.A. Kitchen, *On the Reliability of the Old Testament* (Grand Rapids: Eerdmans Publishing, 2003); Craig Blomberg, *The Historical Reliability of the New Testament* (Nashville: B&H Academic, 2016).

40 *Hidden Figures*. Directed by Theodore Melfi. (Los Angeles: Fox 2000 Pictures, 2016), Film

41 See for a few examples: Isaiah 53, Zechariah 9:9, Micah 5:2, and Psalm 22.

42 Pierre Teilhard de Chardin.

CPSIA information can be obtained
at www.ICGtesting.com
Printed in the USA
FSHW010318180221
78679FS